WORLD
HISTORY SERIES ■ ■ ■

The
Crimean War

Titles in the World History Series

The Age of Augustus
The Age of Feudalism
The Age of Pericles
The Alamo
America in the 1960s
The American Frontier
The American Revolution
Ancient Greece
The Ancient Near East
Architecture
Aztec Civilization
The Battle of the
    Little Bighorn
The Black Death
The Byzantine Empire
Caesar's Conquest of Gaul
The California Gold Rush
The Chinese Cultural
    Revolution
The Civil Rights Movement
The Collapse of the
    Roman Republic
The Conquest of Mexico
The Crimean War
The Crusades
The Cuban Missile Crisis
The Cuban Revolution
The Early Middle Ages
Egypt of the Pharaohs
Elizabethan England
The End of the Cold War
The French and Indian War
The French Revolution
The Glorious Revolution
The Great Depression
Greek and Roman
    Mythology
Greek and Roman Science

Greek and Roman Theater
The History of Slavery
Hitler's Reich
The Hundred Years' War
The Industrial Revolution
The Inquisition
The Italian Renaissance
The Late Middle Ages
The Lewis and Clark
    Expedition
The Mexican Revolution
The Mexican War of
    Independence
Modern Japan
The Mongol Empire
The Persian Empire
The Punic Wars
The Reformation
The Relocation of the
    North American Indian
The Renaissance
The Roaring Twenties
The Roman Empire
The Roman Republic
Roosevelt and the New Deal
The Russian Revolution
Russia of the Tsars
The Scientific Revolution
The Spread of Islam
The Stone Age
Traditional Africa
Traditional Japan
The Travels of Marco Polo
Twentieth Century Science
The Wars of the Roses
The Watts Riot
Women's Suffrage

WORLD
HISTORY SERIES ■ ■ ■

The Crimean War

by
Deborah Bachrach

Lucent Books, P.O. Box 289011, San Diego, CA 92198-9011

In memory of
Uncle Morris and Uncle Issey

Library of Congress Cataloging-in-Publication Data

Bachrach, Deborah, 1943–
    The Crimean War / Deborah Bachrach.
      p. cm. — (World history series)
    Includes bibliographical references and index.
    Summary: A historical overview of the events leading up to,
during, and after the Crimean War.
    ISBN 1-56006-315-7 (alk. paper)
    1. Crimean War, 1853–1856—Juvenile literature. [1. Crimean
War, 1853–1856.] I. Title. II. Series.
DK214.B25   1998
947'.0738—dc21   97-34045
                                                    CIP
                                                      AC

Copyright 1998 by Lucent Books, Inc., P.O. Box 289011,
San Diego, California 92198-9011

Printed in the U.S.A.

Contents

Foreword   6

Important Dates in the History of the
    Crimean War   8

INTRODUCTION
The Setting   9

CHAPTER 1
The Origins of the Crimean War   11

CHAPTER 2
Armies and War Preparations   20

CHAPTER 3
To the Alma and Beyond   33

CHAPTER 4
The Battle of Balaklava   44

CHAPTER 5
The Battle of Inkerman   57

CHAPTER 6
Life in the War Zone   67

CHAPTER 7
The Siege of Sebastopol   80

CHAPTER 8
A Negotiated Peace: Losses and Gains   92

Notes   99
For Further Reading   101
Works Consulted   103
Index   106
Picture Credits   111
About the Author   112

Foreword

Each year on the first day of school, nearly every history teacher faces the task of explaining why his or her students should study history. One logical answer to this question is that exploring what happened in our past explains how the things we often take for granted—our customs, ideas, and institutions—came to be. As statesman and historian Winston Churchill put it, "Every nation or group of nations has its own tale to tell. Knowledge of the trials and struggles is necessary to all who would comprehend the problems, perils, challenges, and opportunities which confront us today." Thus, a study of history puts modern ideas and institutions in perspective. For example, though the founders of the United States were talented and creative thinkers, they clearly did not invent the concept of democracy. Instead, they adapted some democratic ideas that had originated in ancient Greece and with which the Romans, the British, and others had experimented. An exploration of these cultures, then, reveals their very real connection to us through institutions that continue to shape our daily lives.

Another reason often given for studying history is the idea that lessons exist in the past from which contemporary societies can benefit and learn. This idea, although controversial, has always been an intriguing one for historians. Those who agree that society can benefit from the past often quote philosopher George Santayana's famous statement, "Those who cannot remember the past are condemned to repeat it." Historians who ascribe to Santayana's philosophy believe that, for example, studying the events that led up to the major world wars or other significant historical events would allow society to chart a different and more favorable course in the future.

Just as difficult as convincing students to realize the importance of studying history is the search for useful and interesting supplementary materials that present historical events in a context that can be easily understood. The volumes in Lucent Books' World History Series attempt to present a broad, balanced, and penetrating view of the march of history. Ancient Egypt's important wars and rulers, for example, are presented against the rich and colorful backdrop of Egyptian religious, social, and cultural developments. The series engages the reader by enhancing historical events with these cultural contexts. For example, in *Ancient Greece*, the text covers the role of women in that society. Slavery is discussed in *The Roman Empire*, as well as how slaves earned their freedom. The numerous and varied aspects of everyday life in these and other societies are explored in each volume of the series. Additionally, the series covers the major political, cultural, and philosophical ideas as the torch of civilization is passed from ancient Mesopotamia and Egypt, through Greece, Rome, Medieval Europe, and other world cultures, to the modern day.

The material in the series is formatted in a thorough, precise, and organized manner. Each volume offers the reader a comprehensive and clearly written overview of an important historical event or period. The topic under discussion is placed in a broad historical context. For example, *The Italian Renaissance* begins with a discussion of the High Middle Ages and the loss of central control that allowed certain Italian cities to develop artistically. The book ends by looking forward to the Reformation and interpreting the societal changes that grew out of the Renaissance. Thus, students are not only involved in an historical era, but also enveloped by the events leading up to that era and the events following it.

One important and unique feature in the World History Series is the primary and secondary source quotations that richly supplement each volume. These quotes are useful in a number of ways. First, they allow students access to sources they would not normally be exposed to because of the difficulty and obscurity of the original source. The quotations range from interesting anecdotes to farsighted cultural perspectives and are drawn from historical witnesses both past and present. Second, the quotes demonstrate how and where historians themselves derive their information on the past as they strive to reach a consensus on historical events. Lastly, all of the quotes are footnoted, familiarizing students with the citation process and allowing them to verify quotes and/or look up the original source if the quote piques their interest.

Finally, the books in the World History Series provide a detailed launching point for further research. Each book contains a bibliography specifically geared toward student research. A second, annotated bibliography introduces students to all the sources the author consulted when compiling the book. A chronology of important dates gives students an overview, at a glance, of the topic covered. Where applicable, a glossary of terms is included.

In short, the series is designed not only to acquaint readers with the basics of history, but also to make them aware that their lives are a part of an ongoing human saga. Perhaps they will then come to the same realization as famed historian Arnold Toynbee. In his monumental work, *A Study of History*, he wrote about becoming aware of history flowing through him in a mighty current, and of his own life "welling like a wave in the flow of this vast tide."

Important Dates in the History of the Crimean War

| 1853 | 1854 | 1855 | 1856 |

1853

February
Tsar Nicholas I sends Aleksandr Menshikov to Turkey.

April
Canning returns to Turkey.

May
Menshikov leaves Constantinople; Nicholas sends troops to Moldavia.

June
British and French warships near Besika Bay.

July
Russian troops invade Moldavia and Walachia.

October 23
Turkey declares war on Russia.

November 30
Massacre at Sinope.

1854

March
Britain and France declare war on Russia.

April
Allied troops land at Gallipoli.

July 16
Raglan receives letter from London ordering him to fight Russians.

September 14
British and French troops land in the Crimea.

September 20
Battle of the Alma.

October 17–20
First bombardment of Sebastopol.

October 25
Battle of Balaklava.

November 5
Battle of Inkerman.

November 14
Hurricane devastates exposed British troops.

1855

January 24
Fall of the Aberdeen government in London.

March 2
Death of Nicholas I.

April
Destruction of the Flagstaff Bastion.

May
Kerch campaign.

June
Capture of Mamelon and Quarries.

June 29
Death of Lord Raglan.

August 16
Russian attack at the Tchernaya River.

September 5
Sixth bombardment of Sebastopol.

September 10
Russians abandon the south side of Sebastopol; British assault on Redan fails.

1856

January 26
Tsar Alexander II unconditionally surrenders.

March 25
Congress of Paris.

March 30
Treaty of Paris.

The Setting

Lasting from October 1853 to April 1856, the Crimean War was a terrible war. England, France, Russia, Sardinia, and Turkey all suffered tragic losses, both in human and financial terms. The war was particularly tragic for another reason: The slaughter accomplished nothing. It settled few of the issues that initiated the war. The same combatants would soon fight again and even more soldiers would die. Their civilian populations would suffer more carnage and their lands more devastation.

Although the immediate causes of the war are obscure and difficult to explain, the underlying conflict is startlingly clear. Once again a single European power was attempting to establish its domination over the continent.

In the middle of the nineteenth century, Russia's Tsar Nicholas I tried to disrupt the balance of power in Europe by wresting control of the mouth of the Danube River and of the Black Sea from Turkey. The major European powers interpreted Nicholas's attack on Turkey as the first step in a campaign to dominate the entire continent and joined forces to block him.

Russian expansionist efforts did temporarily subside at the conclusion of the Crimean War, but the peace treaty that resulted failed to address the unstable conditions that led to Russia's ability to seize Turkish land. Russia still wanted to control the Black Sea to gain access to the Mediterranean Sea and major trading routes. The Turkish Empire remained weak and unmanageable, and her neighbors greedily eyed various portions of the Turkish sultan's domain.

Battle Tactics

The Crimean War also led to changes in the military. The war highlighted senior officers' inability to develop efficient strategy and tactics, scorning useful techniques such as intelligence gathering on enemy troops before engaging in battle. Britain, especially, also realized that its military equipment was outdated. The following observation by military historian H. A. L. Fisher aptly defines the situation:

> The Crimean War was a contest entered into without necessity, conducted without foresight and deserving to be reckoned from its archaic arrangements and tragic mismanagement rather among medieval than among modern campaigns.[1]

A drawing depicts the fall of Sebastopol. Many soldiers died in the Crimea, both on the battlefield and from exposure and disease.

Faced with undeniable failures, some governments awoke to the need to make drastic changes in their outdated war machines. Others did not, and the widening gaps in military organization and armaments further destabilized the European balance of power.

Changes

In spite of the war's political pointlessness, in addition to military reform it did serve to advance news media coverage of the horrors of the war and the abysmal living conditions of the soldiers in the field. The resulting public outcry helped pave the way for more humane treatment of the common soldier. Knowledge gained during the war led to reforms at home in medical and hospital services and in water purification. There developed an increasingly intense search for and elimination of the causes of diseases such as cholera and dysentery, which killed hundreds of thousands of soldiers. For these and for many other reasons, the Crimean War was an important event in nineteenth-century European history.

1 The Origins of the Crimean War

We were not engaged in any great war for a hundred years after Waterloo. The Crimean War was no exception. It was merely a foolish expedition to the Black Sea, made for no sufficient reason, because the English people were bored by peace.

—Sir George Trevelyan,
English Social History

A series of seemingly minor religious disputes in Palestine eventually led to the outbreak of the Crimean War. Roman Catholic and Greek Orthodox monks had been bickering for years over various rites and relics associated with Christian holy shrines in Jerusalem and Bethlehem. These disputes included control of the key to the Holy Manger and of other doors to the various shrines, the Arches of the Virgin in the Church of the Holy Sepulchre, the Stone of Anointing, and the right to place a glittering silver star in the sanctuary in Bethlehem.

"The Sick Man of Europe"

Ordinarily such quarrels would have been settled as previous similar disputes had been resolved, quietly, through the intervention of the sultan of Turkey. The sultan had final say in such matters because in the middle of the nineteenth century Palestine still belonged to the Turkish Empire. But the mid-nineteenth-century Turkish Empire was weak and decrepit. In fact, in diplomatic circles Turkey was referred to as "the sick man of Europe" because its demise was expected in the not too distant future.

Reeling from economic and political crises, Turkey lurched along under a succession of ineffectual rulers. The current ruler, Sultan Abdul Medjid, was no exception. Yet the empire remained intact largely because of England's economic and political support.

Britain became the protector of Turkey because the sultan controlled the Straits, a series of waterways connecting the Black Sea to the Mediterranean Sea. By befriending Turkey, Britain ensured that the Russian Black Sea fleet, based in Sebastopol on the southwest coast of the Crimean peninsula, could not sail into the Mediterranean Sea where it could threaten the British navy, trade, and security.

Due to his weakening stature, the sultan handled the religious disputes indecisively. At first he decided in favor of the claims of the Roman Catholic monks, bringing jubilation in Catholic countries such as France. Elsewhere, especially in

Russia, it caused intense anger. The Russian tsar, Nicholas I, was infuriated by the sultan's support of the Roman Catholic monks. He believed that the sultan, whom he regarded with contempt, was directly challenging his authority to represent Greek Orthodox religious concerns.

Russian tsar Nicholas I saw the religious dispute in Palestine as an opportunity to wrest control of the Straits from Turkey.

The tsar claimed to protect the interests of the Eastern Orthodox monks. The Russian government then said that it was the tsar's responsibility to protect the religious interests of the 12 million Eastern Orthodox Christians who lived in the European and Asiatic portions of Turkey, by ensuring that they were treated as equals with Muslims.

The Palestinian crisis afforded Nicholas the opportunity both to champion the claims of the Greek Orthodox community in Palestine to the holy shrines and to challenge Turkish control over the Straits, which would gain for Russia access to the Mediterranean Sea.

Britain was quick to condemn any move it perceived as Russian aggression, and British politicians believed it to be in their country's interests to protect the integrity of the Turkish Empire. Russian intervention in Turkish territory in the Balkans, the Black Sea, or the Turkish capitol of Constantinople itself would be viewed as a serious threat.

As the clashes between the monks in Palestine intensified, therefore, Britain attempted to avert a major crisis diplomatically by sending Sir Stratford Canning to Constantinople. Canning was a formidable figure. He had served for many years as British ambassador to Constantinople. He spoke Turkish and he had studied the Koran, the religious book of the Muslim Turks. Through the strength of his own personality and his role in determining British policy in Turkey, he exercised great influence over the sultan. The Turks called him the Great Elchi, or great ambassador. Anxious to avoid giving Russia an excuse for military action, Canning convinced the sultan to change his decision regarding the holy shrines in Palestine to favor the Greek Orthodox monks.

Yet for Russia the decision came too late. With an army of well over a million men, Nicholas appeared on the threshold of fulfilling an expansionist dream he shared with many of his predecessors. Russia was a landlocked giant during the winter months. Nicholas, like earlier Russian rulers, wanted a warm-water port for his country so that Russia could trade year round with the rest of the world. To accomplish his goal, Nicholas wanted to take over the lands bordering the shores of the Black Sea.

The Tsar Sends Menshikov to Constantinople

In February 1853 Nicholas sent his nearly seventy-year-old friend and adviser, Prince Aleksandr Menshikov, to Constantinople to place the new Russian demands before the sultan. Ominously, Menshikov arrived on a ship named the *Thunderer*. Accompanied by a group of high-ranking military officers, the harsh, often outspoken Men-

The British sent Sir Stratford Canning to Constantinople to negotiate the conflict between the Roman Catholic and Greek Orthodox monks.

shikov demanded that the sultan allow the Orthodox monks in Palestine to control the holy shrines.

Then Menshikov dropped his bombshell. Menshikov announced to the sultan that Nicholas represented the nearly 12 million Christians living in Balkan territories such as Serbia, Rumania, and Bulgaria who suffered from religious discrimination under Turkish rule. This "persecution," Menshikov told the sultan, Russia no longer would tolerate. The tsar demanded the right to intervene in Turkey's internal affairs in order to protect the religious and

Nicholas sent Aleksandr Menshikov (pictured) to Constantinople to negotiate with Canning. As a political ploy, Menshikov claimed that the Christians living in Balkan territories were persecuted by the Turks.

political rights of "his" subjects. According to historian Alan Palmer, "It was this demand which brought a long simmering Eastern Crisis to the boil."[2]

Russia's Demands Are Refused

The British government had accepted Russian domination of the affairs of some monks in Palestine, but it could not accept Russia's demand that the tsar intervene in the internal affairs of European Turkey. As Lord Clarendon, the British foreign minister, explained:

> No sovereign, having proper regard for his own dignity and independence, could admit proposals which conferred upon another and more powerful sovereign a right of protection over his own subjects. Twelve millions of Greeks would henceforth regard the Emperor as their supreme protector, and their allegiance to the Sultan would be little more than nominal, while his own independence would dwindle into vassalage.[3]

Emboldened by assurances of protection from the British government, the sultan refused to agree to Menshikov's demands that Turkey turn over control of her Christian subjects to the tsar. Menshikov was furious. To indicate the extent of Russian anger, Menshikov returned to the *Thunderer* on May 21, 1853; with him was the staff of the Russian embassy at Constantinople. He also took the gold Russian eagles that had formally adorned the palatial embassy compound. This was an ominous signal to the European powers.

Tsar Nicholas Moves to Invade

Menshikov reported to an infuriated Nicholas in St. Petersburg. Canning, he informed the tsar, had "bewitched all of Medjid's advisers"[4] and now Russia had to act in its own interests. Nicholas responded by sending two large Russian armies across the Pruth River into the Turkish provinces of Walachia and Moldavia, the future Rumania. He wanted all of Europe to know how seriously he was determined to protect the Eastern Orthodox subjects under Turkish rule.

The sultan, invigorated by signs of British support, demanded that the Russian troops leave Turkish territory. The Russians refused, and the Turks declared war on Russia on October 23, 1853.

The Crisis Spreads

Until 1853 the crisis largely engaged Britain, Russia, and Turkey. Now other European powers began to get involved, recognizing that the conflict offered them opportunities to advance their own interests. France was the most important of these powers.

The emperor of France, Napoleon III, had seized power through a coup d'etat. He was regarded with alarm by other powers of Europe, especially by Britain. France and Britain had been traditional enemies for centuries, and suspicion characterized the relations between the two countries.

The brewing Russo-Turkish crisis provided Napoleon with an opportunity to pursue two of his own goals simultaneously. At home he hoped to gain the support of French Catholics by defending the interests of Roman Catholic monks in Palestine. More importantly, however, he saw political advantage in an alliance with Britain to strengthen his position in France. When Britain challenged Russia's efforts to expand at Turkey's expense, the French emperor made known his support for the Turks and for any diplomatic efforts that Britain might make.

The Tsar Explains His Motives

The tsar invoked religion to explain his reasons for pursuing a military campaign against the Muslim Turks. His quote appears in W. Bruce Lincoln's Nicholas I: Emperor and Autocrat of All the Russians.

"By the grace of God, we Nicholas I, Emperor and Autocrat of all the Russians, make known to our faithful and well-beloved subjects that from time immortal our glorious predecessors took the vow to defend the Orthodox faith. Now, having exhausted all means of persuasion and all means of obtaining in a friendly manner the satisfaction due to our just reclamation, we have deemed it indispensable to order our troops to enter the Danubian Principalities, to show the Port [the sultan of Turkey] how far its obstinacy may lead it. . . . We do not seek conquests. Russia does not need them. We demand satisfaction for a legitimate right only infringed."

Napoleon III of France sided with the British in their conflict with Russia.

But, suddenly, in October 1853 Britain and France found themselves in a terribly awkward position. They were on the verge of an extremely grave international crisis with the mercurial sultan of Turkey directing their foreign policy. The sultan had declared war against Russia without consulting his friends. Though England did not yet feel itself obliged to enter the conflict as a Turkish ally, Queen Victoria acknowledged that "It appears to the Queen that we have taken on ourselves, in conjunction with France, all the risks of a European war." [5]

Peace or War?

Governmental leaders in Britain and France exchanged frantic diplomatic notes

---

Geopolitical Issues at Stake

Historian W. Bruce Lincoln, in Nicholas I: Emperor and Autocrat of All the Russians, *describes some of the geopolitical issues that compelled the governments of England and France to resist Russian attempts at territorial expansion in the 1850s.*

"There was, of course, more to the outbreak of war than simply the failure of diplomatic negotiations. Russia's expanding economic activities in the Near East and Central Asia, and the growing size and power of her fleet, posed a threat to British sea power and imperial economic interests which English statesmen could not ignore. As the French Ambassador to St. Petersburg wrote to his government in Paris, 'Britain has two further interests which we do not share; the destruction of the fleets of all nations [because of the British need to maintain naval superiority] and the diversion of the Russian march toward India [which England controlled at the time].'"

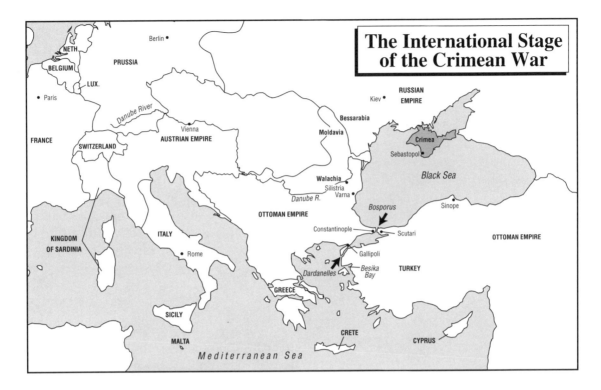

The International Stage of the Crimean War

trying to determine what steps to take. Britain, France, and Russia all tried to enlist the support of Prussia and Austria, either to help avert a general war or to ally themselves with one side or the other.

Meanwhile, the Turks acted on their own. They were faced with the fact of massive Russian armies on Turkish territory. Without the assistance of British or French troops, Turkish armies stubbornly resisted a Russian attack on the fortress of Silistria on the Danube River. This unexpected display of Turkish military ability eventually forced the Russians to reconsider their advance into Turkish territory.

In light of the serious loss of men and matériel, Russian military leaders concluded that they should withdraw their armies from Turkish territory. Russian troops began moving back, beyond the Pruth. Government leaders throughout Europe breathed a collective sigh of relief. They believed that the Russian withdrawal signaled the end of the crisis.

The Massacre of Sinope

Unfortunately, the Russians ineptly provided the excuse for the European war they had until now apparently managed to avoid. In mid-November 1853 the Russian Black Sea fleet under Admiral Paul Nakhimov sailed from its base at Sebastopol to the northern Turkish port of Sinope, only a hundred miles south of Sebastopol but three hundred miles east of the Bosporus, the narrow strait connecting the Black Sea and the Sea of Marmara, where the French and British fleets kept watch on the sultan's palace.

On November 30, 1853, Nakhimov destroyed the entire Turkish fleet at Sinope. More than four thousand people died in the attack and much of the town itself burned to the ground.

The British went wild with fury. England and France had already placed their fleets near the entrance to the Black Sea. Now their citizens were outraged that an attack had taken place while the Turkish fleet was under the protection of the English Royal Navy. The attack on Sinope aroused British national pride in its fleet. Many people in England believed that the Russians were bullies; they rallied around John Bull, the national symbol, to teach the Russian "bear" a lesson.

Newspapers in both Britain and France closely followed the details of the crisis throughout 1853. Now, for the first time in history, public opinion became an important factor in the determination of British foreign policy. The public demanded that something be done to protect unspecified national interests in the Balkans and British and French honor against the Russians. Politicians of both countries feared failure to respond to public outcry might topple their governments. Finally, after many delays, Britain and France declared war

In this political cartoon, Russia, depicted as a bear, grasps Turkey in a stranglehold. Britain and France viewed Russia's actions against Turkey as part of a land grab.

TURKEY IN DANGER.

The Massacre at Sinope

The horrible results of the Russian attack on the Turkish port of Sinope, as described by historian Peter Gibbs in Crimean Blunder, *infuriated public opinion in both England and France and increased their demands for war against Russia.*

"The British and French surgeons, and scores of sympathetic blue jackets, clambered ashore at Sinope over the burnt out hulks on the beach and searched out the cafes and hovels of the town for the terribly mutilated men who lay where they had fallen, or whither they had crawled, dying agonizingly for want of attention. Wounds were painfully and inadequately dressed, and limbs crudely amputated. Those lucky enough also to survive tetanus were at last carried aboard the ships and brought back to Constantinople. At the request of the Turkish authorities the hundreds of wounded were taken ashore during the night in an attempt to conceal from the people of the city the shocking extent of the disaster."

against Russia in March 1854 and prepared to send their armies into battle. Historian Alexis Troubetzkoy comments wryly that "It has been said that the Crimean War has the distinction of taking longer to get itself declared than any war in modern history."[6]

A distant dispute over control of sacred places in Palestine between Roman Catholic and Eastern Orthodox monks had slowly developed into a major European conflict. The lack of diplomatic skill displayed by all sides in the months before the war mirrored the disastrous execution of the conflict itself. Lack of clear military objectives, failure to plan for the war and to supply armies with their basic requirements, as well as a deplorable absence of effective leadership, both civilian and military, led to a human disaster of appalling proportions.

Chapter

2 Armies and War Preparations

For the peace, that I deem'd no peace is
over and done,
And now by the side of the Black and the
Baltic deep,
And deathful-grinning mouths of the
fortress, flames
The blood-red blossom of war with a heart
of fire.

—Alfred, Lord Tennyson, from *Maud*,
written in the spring of 1854

The armies that prepared for battle vastly differed from one another in size, organization, composition, tradition, and experience. In common, however, the soldiers of all the armies displayed remarkable valor throughout the long, grueling war. British, French, Russian, Turkish, and later Sardinian soldiers all demonstrated an extraordinary ability and willingness to endure hardship and privation. They were enormously courageous and showed great devotion to their units and to their leaders.

Unfortunately, these admirable qualities were not matched in the officers who led them or the civilian leaders who sent them off to die on the battlefields of the Crimea or, more often, in unsanitary and ill-staffed army hospitals. A grotesque fact of the Crimean War was that all too often European leaders were unable to keep their soldiers alive long enough to participate in battle.

The Russian Army

Prince Aleksandr Menshikov commanded the Russian army. He was a sixty-seven-year-old political appointee, a crony of the tsar, and he had no experience leading troops. Resistant to compromise, he was temperamentally incapable of accepting advice or criticism, even from senior army officers far more experienced than he. While he could draw on the human resources of an army officially numbering more than a million men, Menshikov quickly demonstrated that sheer numbers were meaningless without effective leadership and shrewd judgment on the part of the high command.

The Russian soldiers Menshikov commanded were drafted into the army for a period of twenty-five years. Not surprisingly, military service was often regarded as a life sentence. Once recruited, often by force, a common soldier rarely if ever returned to his native district or saw his family again.

Most of the Russian army consisted of serfs; that is, peasants legally tied to the land in the service of noble landowners. Serfs were not emancipated by the tsar until 1861. For these soldiers, few differences existed between the hardships of their servitude on the land and their servitude in the army. In either case they could be worked to death by superiors who regarded them as mindless animals who easily could be replaced.

The Russian soldiers were ill trained, poorly armed, or not armed at all. Their officers literally whipped them into a blind, brutish obedience. They endured marches over thousands of miles through country that had almost no railroads and few decent highways. The death rate in the Russian army, even during peacetime, was higher than that of any other army in Europe.

Russian officers were expected never to question an order from a superior. They never acted independently. And they did not challenge the value of their military training, which reduced them to weapons of war.

The only advantage that industrially backward Russia enjoyed against enemies was the massive size of her army. This led to an emphasis on close-range fighting, the use of the bayonet rather than the bullet, and a reliance on assault in column formation, which also favored mass force rather than technical agility. These tactics also were developed because of the crude accuracy of the weaponry of the eighteenth century; a bullet rarely hit its intended mark.

Consequently, casualties were high; soldiers, considered as cannon fodder, received large rations of vodka and brandy as they went into battle, both to lessen their fears and to make them more recklessly brave. Alcohol also numbed their reactions to the sight of the hundreds upon hundreds of their comrades who fell

In an 1855 illustration, Russian citizens are shown being conscripted into the army. Service in the Russian army was a virtual death sentence—few ever returned home to their families.

around them as the gray columns of Russian soldiers rushed toward the ranks of better-armed and better-trained enemy armies. A foe with superior, long-range firepower generally mowed down thousands of Russians long before the Russians could put their bayonets to use.

The Turkish Army

Like the Russian army, the Turkish army consisted of recruits drafted from the far-flung regions of the Turkish Empire. Turks, Egyptians, Tatars, and a variety of ethnic minorities all served under the ruthless, authoritarian rule of their often illiterate Turkish officers. Conscripts and officers alike were largely ignorant of modern military techniques and generally lacked modern weapons.

The Turkish officers had about as much regard for the well-being of their troops as did the Russians. During the war, however, the Turkish army fared somewhat better than the others. It fought closer to home and could receive supplies more easily. The Turks also were accustomed to surviving in the harsh, often widely variable weather of the Crimean region. And they carried with them tents and other supplies that offered more protection from exposure than were provided to their British allies.

The Turkish army also enjoyed the leadership of Omar Pasha. Born in Austria in 1806, he converted from Christianity to Islam and rose rapidly in the Turkish army due to military skill and organizational ability. Omar Pasha eventually became the overall leader of the Turkish forces. He was an exceptional individual in charge of a very backward and poorly trained army.

Historian Peter Gibbs describes graphically just how lacking in general leadership the Turkish army was at the beginning of the Crimean War. He writes that as the Russians began their concentrated invasion of Turkey's European provinces, few Turkish leaders were at the front because many officers were still in school, including

a lieutenant-general, two major generals and a colonel who were struggling with the alphabet in one of the military schools in Constantinople. Admittedly they were still mere youths—all under twenty-one—but they were fortunate enough to have fathers who were ministers of the state.[7]

The British and French viewed the Turkish army with contempt, despite the skilled leadership of Omar Pasha (pictured).

Given the general incompetence of Turkish military and of Turkish leadership at this time, the Turkish troops acquitted themselves remarkably well during the war.

The French Army

The French army was the most professional and experienced of Crimean War combatants. The French had successfully waged a series of colonial wars in North Africa. The army was led by able officers accustomed to hardship and danger. French officers understood the importance of maintaining the morale and the health of their soldiers. The French army was well supplied with modern arms, particularly the exceedingly accurate minié rifle, designed with a spiral-grooved barrel.

General Le Roy de Saint-Arnaud led the French field army, comprised almost entirely of infantry forces. Eventually sixty thousand French foot soldiers served in the Crimean War. When Saint-Arnaud died of cancer early in the war, capable men who had received their training in North Africa under their fallen leader were able to take his place.

The French army was far better fed than any other. The troops arrived with substantial field kitchens. Fresh bread baked in field ovens helped to lighten the otherwise horrible conditions of life at the front. In addition, notes historian Christopher Hibbert, "French soldiers, unlike most English ones, were expert cooks, making delicious dishes from the most unpromising looking rations—from tortoises and even from rats, which they would politely ask permission to catch in Balaclava and take back to their camps impaled on

General Le Roy de Saint-Arnaud, leader of the French army. The French army was the most experienced and well trained of all the forces that fought during the Crimean War.

long sticks."[8] In addition, French soldiers generally slept in tents and received medical treatment from a large corps of medical officers and nurses who accompanied the army to the Crimea.

The British Army

Lord Raglan, who had lost an arm at Waterloo and was an aide-de-camp of the duke of Wellington in 1815, led the British army of twenty-five thousand infantry and twelve hundred cavalry. Lord Raglan, born

Fitzroy Somerset, had spent the past forty years behind a desk at the Horse Guard in London and had never led men in battle. But he was the army's highest-ranking officer, and held an important position at court due to his long-standing relationship with the great Wellington, who lived until 1852.

The British army did boast career professionals who were extraordinarily dedicated and highly motivated to bring honor to their individual units, their queen, and their country. But the army was essentially a parade-ground force in 1854, steeped in tradition and ceremony, trained in the tactics of the Napoleonic Wars of forty years earlier.

British weaponry in this period began to equal that of the French. The British government copied the design of the French minié rifle and stepped up its manufacture at home. Apart from its weapons, however, the British army went to war almost criminally deficient in all of those necessities that might have eased the suffering of its troops in the field.

British forces in the Crimea lacked adequate food supplies, pots and pans, transportation, and appropriate clothing. The government had anticipated a short war. No contingency plans existed to resupply its forces, even as it became apparent that the shortages constituted a major and shameful crisis in war management.

In addition, the War Ministry provided only a minuscule medical staff, supported by male orderlies who had no particular medical training. It was unthinkable to send female nurses to the battlefield, although the French and Russians were not reluctant to do so. There was at the time a belief in England that women who entered the nursing field were no better than pros-

Lord Raglan led the British army. Many high-ranking British officials suffered from inflated egos and treated the soldiers under them with contempt.

titutes, and the high-minded Victorians could not permit such women to tempt the morals of the soldiers.

The officers who served under Raglan generally had seen as little active duty as their leader. For the most part upper class, most had purchased their commissions in the army at very high prices. They viewed their commands simply as fitting reflections of their social status and connections.

British officers believed that mere nobility of birth sufficed as adequate qualification to lead men into battle. Strategic and tactical planning, logistical considerations, questions of supply and resupply were beyond their ken. And, tragically, few appreciated the valiant, brave troops who willingly risked their lives for them. Indeed, the officers barely considered the soldiers human. And the generals who purchased their commissions thought little better of those junior officers who had risen through the ranks and regarded the army as a lifelong profession.

Backward Military Thinking

Although the armies participating in the war varied in many ways, some problems bedeviled the operations of them all. The art of warfare as practiced by the military leaders of the Crimean War reflected ideas of the eighteenth century rather than the nineteenth century, which had become industrialized and highly complex. The older military leaders did not appreciate the power of newly designed guns, mines, artillery, and rapid transportation, which required new tactical and strategic approaches to conflict.

Almost all decision-making power continued to reside in the hands of one or several leaders on the battlefield; not until the very last months of the war did the new invention of telegraphic communication reach from the governments of London and Paris to their military commanders on the Crimean peninsula.

In addition, military leaders and their field staffs continued to wear gorgeously decorated uniforms as they led their troops into battle. They made wonderful targets for enemy snipers and many officers were killed as a result. Since military plans were often not shared with subordinates, the death of such officers frequently led to confusion and heavy casualties on the battlefield among leaderless forces.

Difficulties such as these had always been part of warfare. During the Crimean War, however, these situations became public knowledge: For the first time war correspondents and war photographers accompanied the armies as they prepared for battle. Their reports and photos appeared in the pages of widely read newspapers. Rising popular anger at home, particularly in Britain, against military incompetence began to have an effect on

Photos taken during the Crimean War, such as this one showing a British cookhouse, brought the horrific wartime conditions under public scrutiny.

governments that were used to making foreign policy decisions more or less without scrutiny. Governments inexperienced in managing such wide interest in the war sometimes made unwise decisions guided by fear of losing their popularity at home.

No Clear Plan of Engagement

In the spring of 1854 the armies of Britain and France headed for Turkey with little advance planning. Thousands of troops landed at Gallipoli, not far from Constantinople. But the Russian army was hundreds of miles away along the Danube River. Most of the British generals did not arrive until many weeks after the initial landing of the troops. As they waited for the war to begin, the leaderless soldiers ran short of fresh water, tents, and food, and there was no one with the authority to order these supplies. One British soldier sent a letter to England on April 24, 1854, complaining to his parents about the arrangements:

> On our arrival there [the Dardanelles] we found that only 5,000 English troops had landed, all the rest having been sent on to Scutari. Our arrangements have been infamous; there is no commissariat, the men are half-starved, and officers come on board our steamer to beg for tea, bread, or anything they could get. No generals, except Sir George Brown, have arrived, and no staff. There are no mules for us, in fact, no organization whatever. What a contrast to the French army, which arrived and landed by divisions and brigades with their generals and full staff, commissariat provision mules for everybody, pack-saddles all complete, and ready to march the moment they landed without the slightest confusion.[9]

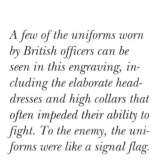

A few of the uniforms worn by British officers can be seen in this engraving, including the elaborate headdresses and high collars that often impeded their ability to fight. To the enemy, the uniforms were like a signal flag.

The British Officer Corps

Cecil Woodham-Smith, in The Reason Why, *provides an example, drawn from the pages of the London* Times, *of the low regard accorded many British military leaders by contemporary opinion makers.*

"How came Lord Budenell [his title before he succeeded his father as Lord Cardigan and led the British cavalry units in the Crimean War]—an officer of no pretensions or experience comparable to those of a hundred other gentlemen who had seen and beaten a foreign enemy—how came such an unripe gallant as this to be put in over the heads of so many worthier candidates, to be forced into a command for which, we may now say, he has proved himself utterly incompetent. This officer was a man of no experience. We are told he never did regimental duty for more than three years of his life. He was not less incapacitated for command by temper, than by ignorance of his duty as a commanding officer, both professional and moral. Such a man ought never to have been placed at the head of a regiment."

Clearly, guarding the approaches to Constantinople was unnecessary since the Russian army had no intention of attacking the Turkish capital and the Russian fleet had returned to Sebastopol after its victory at Sinope in November 1853. In fact, the Russian army soon completely withdrew from all land claimed by Turkey, leaving the allies with no obvious reason for fighting.

The French and the British were stumped. They had no battle plan. The troops scraped along in their very rudimentary camps, living on limited supplies, attempting to deal with polluted water, a dull diet of salted meat, biscuits, and coffee beans with a short daily ration of alcohol to help relieve their discomfort, and boredom. The French soldiers followed much the same daily pattern except that their food was more plentiful and better prepared.

This lack of direction and muddle within the individual armies was further complicated by the failure of the French and British commanding officers to coordinate movements and back each other up in the field during military actions. The French and British governments were similarly uncooperative.

Their past animosities affected their current relationship. The sudden and unusual efforts of the new French emperor, Napoleon III, to ally himself with Britain did not alter the traditional hatred that the soldiers of the two armies maintained for one another. In fact the British soldiers still often used cardboard models of

The Royal Horse Artillery land in Scutari at the onset of the Crimean War. It would be months, however, before the allied officers settled on a plan of attack.

French grenadiers for target practice in their camps. Many British leaders continued to view Napoleon III as an enemy and feared that the modern navy the French built during this period was designed to invade England.

Only a handful of farsighted officers within the two armies, acting outside the chain of command, coordinated efforts during emergencies in an attempt to defeat the Russians. But it seemed the British and the French did share a contempt for the Turkish army in whose defense the war had begun. Both armies regarded the Turks as cowardly barbarians who could not defend themselves and they placed no faith in Turkish military prowess, even though the Turks already had defeated the Russians in battle in 1853 while the allies

had accomplished nothing. This contempt and disdain for the Turks and their military abilities led the allies to ignore valuable information Turkish spies provided regarding Russian troop movements, thereby placing the allied troops in danger unnecessarily.

The Allies Are Ordered to Attack

The allied troops who had arrived in Turkey in the spring of 1854, fresh and eager to fight, remained inactive as spring turned into summer. As the summer heat increased and more and more men succumbed to disease and general neglect,

Lord Raglan knew that he would be forced to explain to his government why the troops had not yet engaged in battle. As historian Alan Palmer writes:

> The mood of anticipatory elation which had gripped the British public in the spring gave way to impatient criticisms of the Government inside and outside Parliament. Everyone wanted to know when the fighting was going to begin.[10]

But a more important question would have been, Where was the fighting going to take place? For the sad fact was that the leaders of the allied armies still had not decided where they would fight the Russian enemy, which had long ago evacuated Turkish territory.

Finally, on July 16, 1854, Lord Raglan received a sharp letter from the government in London. He was ordered to attack Sebastopol, "the City of Imperial Power," the major Russian naval base on the Crimean peninsula. Lord Raglan met with General Saint-Arnaud on July 18 and the two leaders discussed the British government's order.

The French high command agreed to comply with this request. From a military

Before the Fighting Began

Early in the war the British prime minister, the earl of Aberdeen, received disturbing letters regarding the British situation in Scutari from his son, Alexander Gordon, who served with the troops. Historian Alan Warwick Palmer, in The Banner of Battle, *quotes from these letters.*

"May 10, 1854 Gordon to Lord Aberdeen

Nothing is yet known of our ultimate destination or when we are to move, which I fear is not likely to be soon as we have the greatest difficulty in getting baggage animals. Nor a single cavalry officer has yet arrived (with the exception of Lord Lucan)."

Ten days later, on May 30, 1854, Gordon again wrote to his family, this time more shrilly, about the lack of supplies available to the troops:

"We are ready to go up to Varna, but the commissariat is not. They have no horses or mules for the transport of tents, provision and baggage. Instead of setting to work to get them they are engaged in objecting to everything proposed and thwarting Lord Raglan in everything. Until you send out an order that Lord Raglan is to command the army and not the Commissary, General Fielder, we shall not get into ready working order."

point of view it made good sense to fight the enemy at an accessible spot that was an important military objective, as well. They also agreed that it was critical to destroy the Russian Black Sea fleet. By doing so the allies would ensure the security of Turkey and effectively prevent Russia from gaining control of the Straits.

Though Raglan and Saint-Arnaud agreed in principle to follow instructions, they were worried. With good reason: They had no maps of Sebastopol and they knew nothing about the topography of the region they were about to invade. They did not know the strength of the Russian fortifications, nor the size of the Russian army. They had no idea where to land their troops.

Looking for a Landing Site

Allied leaders therefore sailed off on the *Cardoc* to take a first look at the Crimean coastline. They searched for a suitable landing site while their troops remained at Varna, a port on the Black Sea in what is now northeastern Bulgaria. They sailed along the west coast of the Crimean peninsula, in full dress uniforms, with their telescopes pressed to their eyes. Russian lookouts along the coast, telescopes also pressed against their eyes, followed the course of the enemy reconnaissance vessel.

The allied leaders decided that they would land their troops at Calamita Bay, an inlet about forty-five miles north of Sebastopol. Their plan was simple. They would land their troops, march south across the five rivers that separated the landing site from Sebastopol and then attack the Russian naval fortress from the north. Then they would return home before the onset of winter.

Once this strategic decision was reached in early September, Raglan and Saint-Arnaud began the tedious task of loading their weary, often malnourished troops aboard transports. Then the armada sailed off, three hundred miles northeast to the Crimean peninsula and the Russian army that awaited their arrival. Miraculously, the loading took place without major mishap. On September 14, 1854, the allied armies reached Calamita Bay and began to disembark.

Karl Marx Sneers at the Allies

The contemporary economic and social critic Karl Marx also gibed at the allies for their inactivity. Alexis Troubetzkoy, in The Road to Balaklava, *quotes from a newspaper article written by Marx.*

"There they are, eighty or ninety thousand English and French soldiers at Varna, commanded by old Wellington's late military secretary and by a Marshal of France. There they are, the French doing nothing and the British helping them as fast as possible."

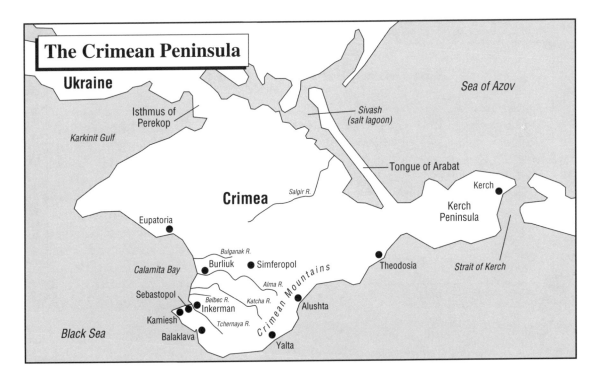

The Crimean Peninsula

Ukraine

Sea of Azov

Isthmus of
Perekop

Karkinit Gulf

Sivash
(salt lagoon)

Tongue of Arabat

Kerch

Crimea

Salgir R.

Kerch
Peninsula

Eupatoria

Bulganak R.

Burliuk

Simferopol

Calamita Bay

Alma R.

Theodosia

Strait of Kerch

Sebastopol

Belbec R.

Katcha R.

Crimean Mountains

Kamiesh

Inkerman

Alushta

Black Sea

Tchernaya R.

Balaklava

Yalta

Getting the troops from Varna across the Black Sea to Sebastopol was one of the greatest triumphs of the war. As historian Peter Gibbs reminds us:

> The sea was certainly calm enough and conditions could not have been better, but in an era of official indecision and incompetence the exercise of actually despatching this great convoy of hundreds of ships stood out as an unfamiliar example of efficient organization. The credit should go to Sir Edmund Lyons [admiral of the British fleet in the Crimean War] who took over the fatherly direction of the convoy.[11]

Now, once again, lack of planning and an absence of basic military knowledge hampered British operations. The French troops generally wore fairly loose-fitting clothing as they stepped or jumped out of their transports. The British were not so fortunate. They were handicapped by their elaborate uniforms, complete with tight belts and trousers, rigid stocks around their necks intended to prevent their heads from turning left or right in parade drill, and heavy hats and boots. Many soldiers, already weakened by disease contracted at Varna, either died in the effort to reach land or fell exhausted on the shore after their strenuous exertions. Their comrades averted their eyes from the many corpses bobbing in the water as the allied troops made their way to land.

A Russian Missed Opportunity

Had the Russian army attacked the disembarking troops on September 14, the invasion force might have been destroyed and the Crimean War would have come to

A British Soldier's View of the Cavalry

The marquess of Anglesey's book, 'Little Hodge,' contains the following letter, written by Lieutenant-Colonel Edward Cooper Hodge, commander of the 4th Dragoon Guards of the Heavy Cavalry, to his wife on August 27, 1854.

"We have not much confidence in our Cavalry General and only hope that he will allow the Brigadiers to move their own Brigades. . . . Lord Lucan is no doubt a clever sharp fellow, but he has been so long on the shelf that he has no idea of moving cavalry, does not even know the words of command, and is very self-willed, and thinks himself right. He has a lot of very indifferent Field Days, which we only hope may have taught him and his staff something, for certainly nobody else has learnt anything."

an abrupt end. At that moment the allied army was completely defenseless. Fortunately for the allies, Russian lack of foresight and misunderstanding of military matters matched their own.

At the head of a large army complete with cavalry forces, Prince Menshikov watched from a safe distance as the enemy began to land. Apparently, it did not occur to him to make an effort to stop them at the water's edge.

That effort, however, would have taken some planning on his part, and the Russian general was not about to change the habits of a lifetime. So Menshikov permitted the allied army to land. Then the allied soldiers—twenty-five thousand British, thirty thousand French, and nine thousand Turks—began the long march toward their destiny and the thirty-eight thousand Russians awaiting their approach.

Chapter

3 To the Alma and Beyond

*The Russians were terrified by the High-
landers whom they referred to as those
savages without trousers.*

—Alan Palmer, *The Banner of Battle*

A series of five small rivers separated the allied army at Calamita Bay from Sebastopol.
Many of the troops were still weak from
cholera and dysentery, which had ravaged
their ranks during their long stay at the
unhealthy camps at Varna. Yet the soldiers
eagerly marched south, anxious to meet
the Russian enemy. Russian scouting par-
ties had been observed watching the allied
landing; the allied troops knew that the
Russian army was not far away.

The allied army crossed the Bulganak,
the first of the rivers, without opposition.
But as they reached the Alma River, on September 20, they knew that Prince Menshikov and his troops were waiting for them.

Setting the Scene

Menshikov carefully selected his battlefield. The Alma River appeared to him to
present a formidable obstacle to the allied
armies. At either bank of the river's mouth
rose a sheer rock face of chalk that Menshikov thought would be impassable. Then

a line of cliffs, some of them almost without tree cover, stretched from the mouth
of the Alma at the Black Sea for many
miles eastward. The cliffs on the southern
bank of the river near the coast seemed to
create a particularly difficult obstacle; they
stood over 350 feet high. Menshikov assumed the allied armies would not be foolish enough to try to scale them in the
absence of a clearly defined pathway.

Instead, Menshikov thought that the allies would attempt to cross the Alma several
miles inland, past the most formidable of
the cliffs. Accordingly, he selected an especially high rise of ground called Kourgane
Hill as his vantage point. From Kourgane
Hill Menshikov could see a great distance
in either direction and therefore could
keep close watch on the advance of the
British, French, and Turkish soldiers.

Menshikov placed a powerful battery
of twelve field guns near the top of the hill.
Russian soldiers then piled earth in front
of the battery to protect the guns from
allied fire as they approached, moving
southward. The extreme strength of the
Russian fortified position led the British to
name it the Great Redoubt.

Menshikov placed most of his army of
approximately thirty-eight thousand troops
in positions around the battery. He
sent only a single battalion of the Minsk

regiment to the mouth of the Alma to guard against a possible enemy flanking action, which in his own mind he had discounted as a possibility.

Then he waited. From the top of Kourgane Hill, Menshikov observed the advance of the allied army toward the north bank of the river. Late on the morning of September 20, 1854, the allied army approached the water's edge. As they looked across the river they saw great gray masses, which they knew to be a huge body of Russian troops waiting for battle. French and British soldiers prepared themselves for action as their leaders tried to decide what to do next.

On that sun-drenched morning Lord Raglan did not yet have a plan of action prepared. According to historian Peter Gibbs, Raglan was a poor military leader:

Raglan objected to planning in principle. He would prefer to decide how the battle should be fought when he was actually facing the enemy—that way he saved himself the need for any concentrated thinking.[12]

Lord Raglan certainly had no idea of the depth of the river he now faced. He did not know how swiftly it ran or where the safest fords could be made.

The British general, however, had one extremely useful piece of information. He had learned a narrow path existed along the sea face of the cliffs on the south bank of the river. The message indicated that a possibility existed that troops could climb this path unobserved by enemy pickets and that they could probably also drag guns to the top of the hill. Once on the top of the hill on the south side of the Alma, the allies could begin a surprise flanking attack against the left wing of the Russian army while the main army crossed the river farther upstream.

Raglan and Saint-Arnaud met to consider their options. They decided that part of the French army would cross the Alma near its mouth, climb the cliffside path, and surprise the Russians on their left flank. Raglan hoped, but drew no assurances from Saint-Arnaud, that the French diversion would develop into a full-scale at-

Animosity Between British Cavalry Leaders

From the beginning of the campaign, the British cavalry leaders' hatred for one another threatened to disrupt the army. In Crimean Blunder, *Gibbs describes the situation.*

"The British cavalry came upon two thousand Russian cavalrymen standing ranged in line across a ridge over the Bulganak River. Cardigan wanted to charge. Lord Lucan ordered him not to. The Russian cavalry, perplexed by the spectacle of the entire motionless enemy sitting quietly on their horses while their commanders argued, obligingly sat still themselves to await the outcome of the dispute."

tack, drawing Russian troops away from Kourgane Hill, where the British planned to stage a major assault against the powerful Russian position at the Great Redoubt.

The British army, splendid in its bright red uniforms, gold buttons and decorations gleaming in the sunshine, waited on the north bank of the Alma River. The bright afternoon sun blazed on them. Their officers, in full dress, plumed feathers in their hats, rode at the front of their lines. All made excellent targets for the Russian guns across the river. The Russians began to fire volleys from the hill to get the enemy's range. While most of the shells fell short, enough hit their marks for the British officers to order their men to lie down in the grass to reduce their visibility and vulnerability.

The Battle of the Alma

Meanwhile, a small party of Frenchmen led by General Pierre Bosquet made its way down the bank of the Alma. At the mouth of the river the Frenchmen discovered a place shallow enough to cross safely to its south bank. Then they began cautiously to climb up the narrow sea face path, even managing to drag some field pieces to the top of the cliff.

The Russian guards were completely surprised by the appearance of the French soldiers. Immediately they understood the danger presented by this flank attack. One officer recovered his wits sufficiently to send an urgent message to Prince Menshikov alerting him to the enemy's presence on the south side of the river. The Russians did not realize that the small force had no backup.

Three miles away, at the crest of the Kourgane Hill, Prince Menshikov received the news with astonishment and horror. In a panic, he hastily assembled seven battalions of infantry, two batteries of guns, and a squad of cavalry and rode off in a frenzy in the direction of the coast to destroy the French troops.

The rest of the Russian army, under General V. I. Kiriakov, "to whom," according to historian Alan Palmer, "sobriety came as an unnatural condition,"[13] remained to face the enemy. Menshikov left no orders for Kiriakov when he flew off toward the coast. Untrained to take the initiative, now filled with trepidation, and with no specific plan of action, Kiriakov faced the British army, which began to stir in anticipation of a diversion downriver from their French ally.

But the expected massive French attack never materialized. Without informing Raglan, Saint-Arnaud decided that he would only risk a handful of his men on the secondary action. Nevertheless, after waiting for several hours, Raglan decided to move across the river even without the diversion of a major French attack on the Russian army. Raglan instructed his aide, Captain Lewis Edward Nolan, to pass along the word to the brigadiers in charge of the five British infantry divisions, lined up along a length of six miles of the riverbank, that the attack would proceed.

Anticipating Raglan's order, Colonel Sir Colin Campbell, commander of the Highland Scots regiment, and a thirty-four-year veteran of military campaigns, decided independently that actual battle would not be long postponed. With the sun beating down on him and his men, Campbell told the Highlanders to make ready some of their cartridges. According to historian Peter Gibbs, "The thought had so far occurred to no one that they might be as near to battle as that and when the Highlanders started opening their pouches the whole army followed suit."[14]

Finally the British troops received the order to advance. Even the British units directly in the line of fire of the massed Russian guns on Kourgane Hill rose in a disciplined line and began to march down to the river in the face of enemy fire, their officers at their head. Russian shells fell among their ranks. The red-coated soldiers marched on, those still standing after each deadly enemy volley hurrying to fill in the holes left in the ranks by their fallen comrades. Officers continued to urge the soldiers toward the enemy that awaited them across the river.

One Russian soldier who witnessed the advance of the British at the Alma reported his admiration for the thin line marching toward the Russian position:

> As the enemy got closer our shells began to blow great holes in his ranks; but the many gaps were immediately closed up and the enemy strode on, apparently indifferent to his losses. Soon afterwards we began to feel the terrible effects of his rifle fire.[15]

Down into the Alma River the British soldiers marched, across the river they went, and then, protected by the southern cliffs, up the south side of the riverbank they climbed, moving ever closer to the enemy and to the deadly fire of its cannon. Sounds of rifle shots, the roar of cannon, and the agonized cries of the wounded and dying filled the air.

Fortunately, the British troops received some cover from the smoke and fire of allied guns on the north bank of the river. Ironically, they were aided still more by the smoke of fires set by the enemy. Units of the Cossack cavalry had torched Burliuk, a Tatar village lying to the east of the Russian artillery emplacements. But instead of blocking the enemy advance as intended, the smoke now blew back into the faces of the Russian artillerymen and partly obscured their sight.

Brigade-General Sir William Codrington and his men emerged first from the river and tried to fight their way up to the Russian guns. Despite sustaining considerable losses the remnants of the division raced toward the Great Redoubt, with Codrington on his white pony in the lead. As they neared their goal, they suddenly saw two huge massed Russian columns emerge from behind the gun emplacements to join with the artillerymen already there. Possibly ten thousand Russian infantry now confronted the bloodied division head on.

The Tide of Battle Turns

Codrington's men were forced to retreat. But just then the Light Division under Sir George Brown also threw itself against the Russian guns of the Great Redoubt. The great Russian masses pressed hard against the greatly outnumbered British, and Sir George decided to halt his attack.

Fortunately, just at that moment Guards units and the Highlanders also appeared over the cliffs. They immediately joined forces with the soldiers of the First Division under the duke of Cambridge and began to reinforce the efforts of Codrington's and Sir George Brown's men to establish their position at the Great Redoubt.

Colin Campbell Prepares His Men for Battle

Christopher Hibbert describes Colonel Colin Campbell preparing his men for the Battle of the Alma in The Destruction of Lord Raglan.

"As he waited with members of the 93rd Highlanders for the Battle of the Alma to begin he warned his men of their duty. 'Now men, you are going into action. Remember this; whoever is wounded—I don't care what his rank is—whoever it is must lie down where he falls till the bandsmen come to attend to him. No soldiers must go carrying off wounded men. If any soldier does such a thing his name shall be struck up in the parish church. Don't be in a hurry about firing. Your officers will tell you when to do so. Be steady. Keep silent. Fire low.'"

Unlike most British officers, who attained their positions by social class, Sir Colin Campbell earned his rank through years of military experience.

The Russians had never seen the extended British line marching. They assumed that many more men followed behind the two ranks of the Highlanders in their tall hats and kilts.

The Russians at the Great Redoubt now felt the tide of battle turning against them. Their most urgent concern became the need to protect their guns from capture: Tsar Nicholas believed that the heroic duke of Wellington in his wars against Napoleon I never had relinquished any of his field pieces to the enemy, and had fashioned this myth into an obligation on his army.

The Russian officers at Kourgane Hill that day knew that there would be a terrible price to pay if any Russian guns were captured by the British army while Prince Menshikov was off fighting near the cliffs.

At all costs they had to protect the guns from falling into the hands of the British who now swarmed toward them over the battlefield.

The gunners quickly began to remove the field pieces. The Russian infantry, greatly outnumbering the British and arranged in eight huge columns, formed a protective screen for the guns. The Russians attacked the greatly outnumbered British.

The British held. Still in line formation, scarcely more than two men deep, they turned slightly to meet the oncoming Russian army. As a result of this shift in direction, the massed columns of Russians

---

Prince Menshikov

Prince Aleksandr Menshikov commanded the Russian forces in the Crimea at the beginning of the war. Historian Christopher Hibbert, in The Destruction of Lord Raglan, *provides a description of the man that helps to explain why he was such an unsuccessful leader.*

"He was by nature a confident man. Arrogant and autocratic, he was not popular with his men; and his officers had long since learned not to offer him any advice. In a previous campaign he had been castrated by a round of shot from a Turkish gun, and he hated the Turks, and all their allies, with a hatred pathological in its intensity. His headquarter on Kourgane Hill overlooked what he hoped would be the scene of their slaughter."

Prince Aleksandr Menshikov had no experience leading troops, and he proved to be a poor leader. His poor character did not improve after the Crimean War—he was eventually sent to Siberia by the tsar for his misdeeds while in the government.

The Highlanders advance during the Battle of the Alma. The Highlanders joined forces with the failing British troops and forced the Russians to retreat.

faced the British on the oblique. This meant that a maximum number of Russian soldiers were exposed to the precision rifle fire of the British miniés at extremely close range. The result was deadly.

The thirty-five-year-old duke of Cambridge, first cousin to Queen Victoria, ordered his soldiers to advance on the center of the Russian army, firing their guns as they went. On came the British soldiers, firing murderous volleys at the Russians. The Russian massed columns wavered under the deadly hail of the British volleys, halted, and then began to retreat.

Defeat at the Alma

The Russian retreat led from one ridge of hills to another, gathered speed, and finally became a full-scale rout as the Rus-

sian soldiers threw down their equipment and fled south toward the safety of Sebastopol. Discarded guns, ammunition cases, and the bodies of the wounded and dying marked the path of the fleeing army.

The allied armies had won their first encounter with the Russians, but the victory was modest. Moreover, although the British and French could not foresee the future, the characteristics of the Battle of the Alma, unfortunately, presaged all the battles of the Crimean War. There were no great generals leading their armies. There were no brilliant military strategists who carefully planned actions to maximize the use of terrain, light, and weather conditions. Enemy blunders rather than British and French expertise determined the outcome of the battle.

Instead, only the loyal and disciplined soldiers, despite lack of judgment and expertise in their commanders, fought

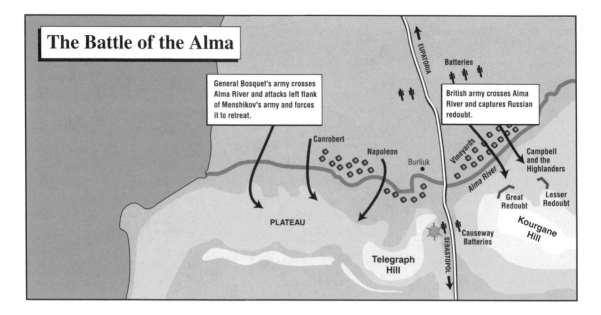

The Battle of the Alma

General Bosquet's army crosses Alma River and attacks left flank of Menshikov's army and forces it to retreat.

British army crosses Alma River and captures Russian redoubt.

Batteries

Canrobert

Napoleon

Burliuk

Vineyards

Campbell and the Highlanders

Alma River

Great Redoubt

Lesser Redoubt

PLATEAU

Causeway Batteries

Kourgane Hill

EUPATORIA

SEBASTOPOL

Telegraph Hill

valiantly and died wretchedly on those battlefields. Historian Cecil Woodham-Smith provides a striking condemnation of the leaders of the armies:

> It was a battle forever memorable for the ferocious courage of the British troops and the extraordinary incompetence displayed by the generals on both sides. What has been called the characteristic insanity of the Crimean War reached its height at the Alma. Advantages were gained not through superior skill, but as a result of astonishing blunders made by each participant in turn; and the victory, won after a desperate and bloody struggle, was attributable solely to the fighting qualities of the British soldiers. In the Battle of the Alma the cavalry played no part. Furious and resentful, it was their fate to sit motionless in their saddles, onlookers once more.[16]

The cost of that display of courage was very high. After the battle, 2,000 British soldiers, 5,700 Russians, and 550 French soldiers lay wounded or dead on the battlefield.

There also continued a wasteful lack of unity between the heads of the British and French forces. The failure of the French to support the British action at the Alma angered Lord Raglan. The great difference in the number of allied casualties spoke volumes on that score.

Now a second major dispute arose. Lord Raglan wanted to pursue the fleeing Russians and attempt to destroy Menshikov's forces before they reached the safety of Sebastopol.

Raglan begged Saint-Arnaud in vain to join in the British effort. Regretfully, Raglan decided that he would not pursue the Russians on his own and destroy what little unity existed in the allied war effort.

Instead, two precious days passed before the allied army resumed its march toward Sebastopol. During that respite Menshikov and his troops had time to regroup within the safety of the forts protecting Sebastopol: At his leisure Menshikov decided his next steps.

Then, one of the most bizarre episodes in the annals of military history occurred. In the face of a victorious enemy army descending upon its main military objective, the great naval port of Sebastopol, the military commander in charge of defending the port abandoned it. Aleksandr Menshikov left Sebastopol virtually defenseless. At the end of September only three or four thousand sailors from the Black Sea fleet were left to defend the port and the civilian population behind Sebastopol's crumbling land defenses.

Menshikov had decided to withdraw toward the interior of the Crimean peninsula. Believing the invading army would

not follow him, he apparently decided that it was important to protect his supply line from the east Crimean port of Kerch.

British and French Ports of Supply

Menshikov was spared the consequences of an unwise decision by the equally inexplicable determination of the allies to avoid victory when it was within their grasp. The allied armies could have descended upon undefended Sebastopol and taken it almost without a fight at the end of September 1854. Instead, the British and French armies circled to the south of

Medics aid a dying man on the battlefield after the Battle of the Alma. Many soldiers died, victims of their incompetent and headstrong leaders.

Sebastopol until they reached ports where their ships could dock and supplies could be off-loaded.

Lord Raglan stopped at the tiny port of Balaklava, about six miles from Sebastopol. Because Raglan believed that the campaign against the Russians would be short, he decided that the extremely small size and limited facilities of Balaklava would suffice as the major British port of supply.

The French army continued its march farther to the west. Ten miles along the coast Saint-Arnaud found two larger ports, Kamiesh and Kazatch, which the French general decided would adequately serve the needs of the French army for its short stay in the Crimea.

A Squandered Opportunity

As a result of this strange series of decisions, military leaders lost the opportunity to end the Crimean War quickly and without the cost of hundreds of thousands of casualties and great and lasting international bitterness. Instead, the sad and weary drama of the Crimean War began to unfold. Aleksandr Menshikov soon re-

Lord Raglan decided to use the tiny port of Balaklava as the main supply port for the British army during the Crimean War.

Lack of Strategic Planning

One of the major criticisms of the allied leaders was their failure to define their objectives in a clear and systematic manner. Peter Gibbs captures allied confusion regarding their military goals in the following quotation from his book Crimean Blunder.

"The French were reluctant to land anywhere near Sebastopol itself but it was clear enough now that with sixty thousand troops gathered a few miles from the enemy coast, some decision had to be made about where they were to land. Not that it appeared to cause much concern to anybody that the objective of the whole expedition, the investment and capture of Sebastopol after the armies had been landed had never even been considered in detail. The only problem before the staff at present was to get the troops off the ships and on the land, and although Sir Edmund Lyons [the naval commander] had already made a reconnaissance of the coast and had chosen a landing place, Lord Raglan decided to do it all over again.

They had no idea yet whether they would land their forces north or south of Sebastopol, nor had they any preference so long as they could get them ashore somewhere, for no consideration at all had been given to the manner in which the long-anticipated assault on the town was eventually to be launched."

turned to Sebastopol to help rebuild its fortifications. Lord Raglan and the French general François-Certain Canrobert, who took over command of the French army when Saint-Arnaud died, realized that hope for a speedy capture of Sebastopol had disappeared.

Depression began to settle on the allied forces. What they and their governments had anticipated would be a short campaign, ending before bad weather returned to the Crimea, now appeared to be taking on the proportions of a major and lengthy military undertaking.

In the Russian camp, however, spirits rose. Sebastopol defenses grew stronger every day. Menshikov, who returned to Sebastopol on September 30, now envisioned a single major action by which he could drive the demoralized allied army out of the Crimea.

He decided to attack the British army. Both Menshikov and the tsar believed that if the British were driven out of the war, the French and Turks soon would follow. So Menshikov prepared his army to attack the British at their weak point, the lightly defended port of Balaklava.

4 The Battle of Balaklava

Theirs not to reason why,
Theirs but to do and die:
Into the valley of Death
Rode the six hundred.

—Alfred, Lord Tennyson,
"The Charge of the Light Brigade"

The Battle of Balaklava, or more exactly, the four actions that together constitute the Battle of Balaklava, occurred on October 25, 1854. The encounter took place within a relatively small area. The two sides fought on uneven lowlands stretching between a crest behind the British supply port of Balaklava and a series of steep hills and gorges rising to the north and west of the port and leading eventually to the high ground above Sebastopol, six miles away. This fairly level area is called the Balaklava Plain.

Lord Raglan Takes Steps to Defend Balaklava

Lord Raglan appreciated the importance of defending Balaklava, his supply base, from a surprise attack. Loss of the port would be a catastrophe for the British war effort. So Raglan ordered that a number of small defensive positions—some gunnery units up in the hills, some cavalry units in the foothills near the entrance to the port—be established as part of an outer ring of defenses. He hoped that together they would be strong enough to repel the early stages of a Russian attack.

The main body of British troops continued to hold their positions in the hills above Sebastopol, thus overlooking the naval port to the northwest. If Raglan's small defensive units were attacked, their task was to hold their positions until military units from the larger force came to their assistance.

The Redoubts

Among the key components of the defensive system established by Lord Raglan was a series of hastily erected miniature redoubts. These were primitive earthworks, or earthen fortifications, which were built at intervals of about half a mile atop a ridge called the Causeway Heights. The Heights separated the North and South Valleys of the Balaklava Plain. Turkish soldiers, commanded by British officers and fortified by British twelve-pound naval guns, defended these outposts.

Lord Raglan had little respect for the military skills of the Turkish soldiers. Necessity, however, compelled him to use them to man the redoubts. His own army was too small and too weakened by disease simultaneously to defend these exposed positions and keep watch over the Russian forces in Sebastopol. Consequently, about one thousand Turkish soldiers stood guard in the redoubts, watching the surrounding landscape for signs of an approaching enemy.

Lord Raglan should have paid more attention to the special skills of the Turkish soldiers. Among them were expert spies who displayed a wonderful ability to penetrate the outposts of the Russian forces. Turkish spies learned that the Russian army was to make its way through the mountain passes to the north of Balaklava before the sun rose on October 25 and launch a surprise attack on the British positions along the Causeway Heights.

Lord Raglan viewed the use of spies, especially Turkish spies, as beneath the dignity of a British officer and gentleman. He failed to heed Turkish warnings to establish stronger watches and strengthen the redoubts. When the attack began, Raglan and his immediate staff were indeed surprised. They were safe and asleep, several miles away, on the Sapoune Heights overlooking the Balaklava Plain when the battle began.

Historians such as Cecil Woodham-Smith have criticized Raglan for his lack of preparedness that day:

> Raglan was unprepared for the attack on Balaclava which was undertaken on the 25th of October, by a Russian army of about 25,000 men. The forces had been concentrating for some time and were under the orders of General [Pavel] Liprandi. With a large enemy force preparing, within six miles, to attack a weakly-defended position and a vital base, there was no systematic reconnaissance, no careful posting of picquets [pickets] or vedettes [mounted sentinels].[17]

Fortunately, the Russian attack did not come as a complete surprise to several high-ranking officers in charge of the defensive operations of the British army. Lord Lucan, commander of the cavalry forces, and Sir Colin Campbell, in charge of the 93rd Highland Regiment, felt restless on that chill October morning. Accompanied by several aides, they decided to ride out together to review the military situation on the Balaklava Plain while it was still dark.

With the first rays of morning light they saw that not one but two flags were flying

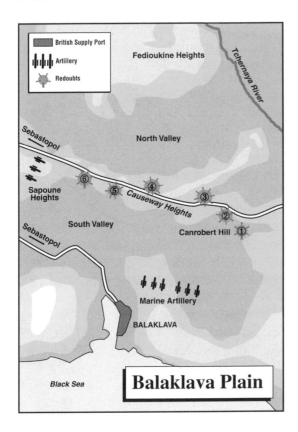

Balaklava Plain

atop the most remote of the redoubts, Canrobert Hill. Two white flags signaled that the defenders of the redoubts were under attack by the Russians. And indeed, at that very moment, several thousand Russian cavalry, part of the attack force of twenty-five thousand Russians, began to fire on the Turks who manned the first line of defense.

Although they were vastly outnumbered, the Turkish soldiers fought bravely that morning. They held out, expecting assistance from the British momentarily. But assistance never came. In the confusion that followed the start of the early morning attack, the British high command never attempted to relieve the Turks, who suffered terrible losses—more than half their number were either dead or wounded by the end of the attack.

As their numbers dwindled, further resistance became futile. The surviving Turkish soldiers grabbed the few personal items they could carry and ran for their lives from the redoubts toward Balaklava. The Russian cavalry pursued them, cutting down the slowest of the retreating Turks with their sabers. A few Turkish soldiers managed to make their escape to the port. Some took part in its defense.

Scrambling to Defend Other Positions

The many Turkish lives lost holding out against the Russians provided the British a precious hour and a half to prepare a defense. During that time Lord Lucan rushed back to alert his own cavalry units, which were stationed at the base of the Sapoune Heights, at the end of the valley.

The cavalry division included two brigades, distinguished by the size of their horses and arms. The Heavy Brigade, un-

Trapped in the Redoubts

In his book The Invasion of the Crimea *historian and reporter A. W. Kinglake explains why the Turkish soldiers in the redoubts built to defend Balaklava did not get assistance on the morning of October 25, 1854.*

"Sir George Cathcart was ordered by Raglan's staff officer to move immediately to the help of the Turks. Cathcart told him that it was 'quite impossible, Sir, for the 4th Division to move.' The staff officer replied that 'My orders were very specific and the Russians are advancing upon Balaclava.' Cathcart replied, 'I can't help that Sir, it is impossible for my Division to move since the greater portion of the men have only just come from the trenches. The best thing you can do is to sit down and take some breakfast with me.' A short time later some bugles sounded and the division began its slow descent to the Balaclava Plain."

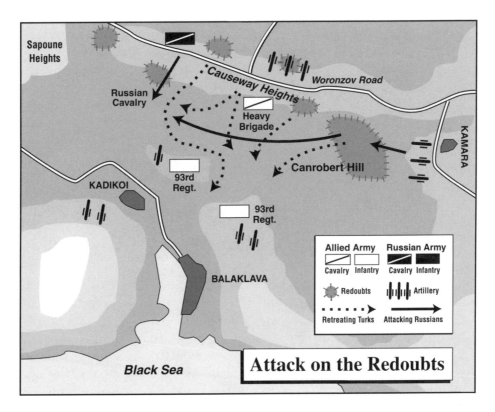

Attack on the Redoubts

der the direction of General Sir James Scarlett, carried swords and carbines and directly opposed enemy cavalry in the thick of battle. The Light Brigade, led by Lord Cardigan, carried lances on smaller, lighter horses, and generally engaged in scouting and skirmishes. As soon as he received news of the attack on the redoubts, Scarlett began to prepare his cavalry for action. Cardigan, however, still slept peacefully aboard his private yacht in Balaklava harbor. Lord Lucan assigned another officer, Sir George Paget, to prepare the troops of the Light Brigade for action.

Meanwhile Sir Colin Campbell, who had been with Lucan, rushed back to prepare his own kilt-clad Highlanders. Their job was to defend the critical position in front of the road leading down to the port. He commanded a mixed group of about four hun-

dred soldiers, comprising fierce Scot warriors from the 93rd Regiment and small units of Turkish soldiers whose ranks were soon swelled by the surviving Turkish soldiers from the redoubts. Even some invalid British soldiers dragged themselves up from their sickbeds in Balaklava itself to make what appeared to be an impossible stand against the approaching Russian cavalry.

The Defense of the 93rd

The British and Turkish soldiers took up their positions near the crest of the road that led down to the port of Balaklava and prepared to take a stand against an equal number of Russian cavalry, energized by their victory over the Turks in the redoubts.

Members of the Highlanders hold the line, bayonets aloft, as the Russians attack. The Highlanders successfully defended their position during the Battle of Balaklava.

Campbell moved his men slightly rearward, to the far side of a small hillock. He wanted to minimize his troops' exposure to the guns fired at the remnants of the fleeing Turks. Then, just as he had done before the Battle of the Alma on September 20, Campbell again ordered his men to lie down in the grass as a further protective measure. He also wanted to disguise the size of his defending infantry force as long as possible. As they waited for the Russian attack Campbell spoke to his men. "Remember there is no retreat from here, men! You must die where you stand." The men cheered his appeal, answering, "Ay, Ay, Sir Colin, we'll do that."[18]

As the Russian cavalry charged the British position, Campbell ordered his men to rise. He directed them to advance to the top of the hill in line formation to receive the oncoming thrust of the charge. The Russians paused momentarily; Campbell, seeing the eagerness of his men to run forward, shouted at them to keep their places: "93rd! 93rd! Damn all that eagerness."[19]

With the enemy still four hundred yards distant, the Highlanders fired a first round. Only a handful of bullets reached the Russian horsemen. At one hundred yards a far more deadly British volley staggered the Russian ranks.

The Russian commander responded by changing the direction of the attack. He ordered his troops to move against the Highlanders from an oblique angle on their flank. But Campbell, one of the few experienced senior soldiers in the British army, shifted his own thin red line so that his left wing suddenly became his front. By taking this action, all of the British soldiers faced the Russians head on, thus minimizing the effectiveness of the Russians' attempt to destroy the Highlanders and the immensely important port they defended.

Retreat of the Russian Cavalry

The Russian horsemen turned around and rode back over the Causeway Heights to join the main body of the Russian army. Overjoyed, the Highlanders shouted hurrahs into the morning air. On the top of the Sapoune Heights, Lord Raglan, his entourage, and a number of newsmen were likewise elated.

Their momentary pleasure suddenly changed to grave anxiety and then to horror as the British command watched the drama unfolding 350 feet below their own position. Illuminated by the bright early morning sunlight, the spectators had a clear view of the action on the Balaklava Plain, divided into the North and the South Valleys with the Causeway Heights rising between.

They could see Sir James Scarlett calling the Heavy Brigade into battle formation. He had a difficult time; the debris of the cavalry camp—tents, ropes, and gear—entangled the legs of both the horses and men of the brigade.

Collision Course

What Raglan could see but Scarlett, attempting to lead the Heavy Brigade along the foot of the Heights, could not was huge numbers of Russian cavalry advancing on a collision course at that very moment. The Russians neared the top of the Heights on their way into the South Valley. The clash of the two forces was imminent. Lord Raglan could not warn the brigade; he was too far away and had no means of communication.

Suddenly, Lieutenant Alexander James Hardy Elliot, aide to Scarlett and riding at the general's side, caught the glint off the tips of the lances of the as yet invisible Russians from the other side of the hill. Immediately he alerted Scarlett to the danger. The Russians appeared ominously at the top of the Heights, and Scarlett called a halt of his own cavalry. With meticulous attention to detail, General Scarlett ordered the Heavy Brigade to line up in battle formation.

The Russians, instead of charging, halted, as well, inexplicably giving the British time to prepare for battle.

Preparing the Heavy to Charge

Woodham-Smith's The Reason Why *captures the anxiety of the British observing the Heavy Brigade in the moments before the charge began.*

"To watchers on the heights, the delay was all but unendurable. Three hundred troopers only formed Scarlett's first line and they were occupied moving a few feet this way or that while a grey torrent of horsemen, appearing all the more irresistible for its deliberate measured pace descended upon them. Suddenly the unbelievable happened. . . . Russian trumpets sounded, the great mass of horsemen came to a halt and proceeded to throw out two wings from the central square in order to outflank the British."

The Charge of the Heavy Brigade

Scarlett made certain that the horses and men of the Heavy Brigade stood in proper battle formation. The Russians meanwhile spread out atop the hill in a crescent formation, in their concentration very dark and very formidable. Satisfied with his brigade's arrangement, Scarlett turned to face the huge, menacing crescent spread out before him.

Until this moment, the fifty-five-year-old Scarlett had never led men in battle. He would have been entirely within military rights to turn over the actual charge to a junior officer. Instead, he exhibited extraordinary bravery on that October morning.

Scarlett raised his sword, rode out ahead of his men and charged, uphill, into the center of the waiting Russian cavalry. Historian John Sweetman describes the excitement that filled the British high command:

> To the spectators on the Sapoune Ridge, the scene was pure theatre. Elliot in his cocked hat rode beside Scarlett, who wore a blue frocked coat and burnished helmet rather than a general's headdress. Slightly behind them rode a solitary trumpeter and Scarlett's massive orderly, Shegog.[20]

The first ranks of the Heavy Brigade followed; from the top of the Sapoune Heights the British command saw the small force of red vanish into the sea of gray. Then the wings of the crescent folded

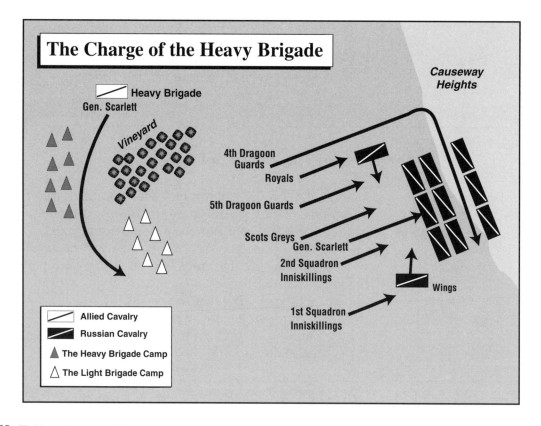

The Charge of the Heavy Brigade

Causeway Heights

Heavy Brigade
Gen. Scarlett

Vineyard

4th Dragoon Guards
Royals
5th Dragoon Guards
Scots Greys
Gen. Scarlett
2nd Squadron Inniskillings
1st Squadron Inniskillings

Wings

Allied Cavalry
Russian Cavalry
▲ The Heavy Brigade Camp
△ The Light Brigade Camp

General Scarlett leads the Heavy Brigade against the Russians at Balaklava, causing the Russians to retreat despite their overwhelmingly favorable odds.

in to envelop the men General Scarlett had led into battle. The Heavy Brigade appeared to vanish.

But then the two remaining ranks of the Heavy charged uphill into the enveloping wings of the Russian cavalry. Those atop the Heights held their breath. It seemed impossible that the brigade could survive that crush. Then suddenly, from the far end of the great mass of men and horses, Scarlett emerged, his red face and distinctive white mustache visible to the watchers on the hill, his sword still held high. The larger, heavier horses of Scarlett's troops simply overwhelmed the Russians. The massed Russian cavalry appeared to heave this way and that, then began to retreat, back over the Causeway Heights and into the North Valley of the Balaklava Plain.

The entire action lasted less than ten minutes. The British sustained 78 casualties, a miraculously low count in view of their disadvantage in numbers. The Russians suffered the loss of 550 men. They were thrown into disorder and began to ride away, briefly pursued by the small force of the Heavy Brigade until officers halted the counterattack.

There were high spirits in the allied camp. True, the Turks had been driven from the redoubts on the Causeway Heights. Yet it seemed that the British had much to celebrate that morning. They had thwarted the Russian attempt to attack Balaklava and General Scarlett, and the Heavy Brigade had driven the Russian cavalry into the North Valley, handing them their second defeat of the day.

One person in the British camp was not altogether pleased with the success of the Heavy Brigade. Lord Cardigan did not share in the celebration. Refreshed by a comfortable night's sleep aboard his yacht, Cardigan sat glumly at the head of the troops of the Light Brigade. Cardigan was eager for his own share of glory. Instead he remained inactive. His much detested brother-in-law and superior officer, Lord Lucan, sent him no message to join the fray.

Eager for Action

Lord Cardigan had not enjoyed the war. He hated being in a position inferior to that of his brother-in-law. The relations between the two nobles became so strained that they threatened to undermine the ability of the British cavalry to operate successfully.

Thus far, Cardigan had seen almost no action. He yearned to show the world what he could do, despite the fact that he, like his counterpart in the Heavy Brigade, had never led men in battle.

But unlike Scarlett, Cardigan lacked insight, judgment, and balance. Arrogantly, he rejected the advice of those he considered his inferiors. On October 25, 1854, those character flaws led him into one of the most horrific military actions in all of British history.

The awful event began when Lord Raglan, looking down from the Heights onto the plain, saw that the Russian cavalry, carrying ropes and other equipment, was removing from the redoubts the guns that the Turks had abandoned. The Russians intended to take them back to Se- bastopol as trophies of war. They believed that military activity had ended for the day.

Protecting British Guns

Raglan was incensed by the weapons capture. He quickly issued an order to Lord Lucan:

Lord Raglan wishes the cavalry to advance rapidly to the front, follow the enemy and try to prevent the enemy carrying away the guns. Troops of horse artillery may accompany. French cavalry is on your left. Immediate.[21]

The penciled note, scrawled on a scrap of brown paper, was signed not by Raglan but by his quartermaster-general, General Sir Richard Airey.

Captain Nolan, Raglan's aide-de-camp, delivered the note to Lord Lucan, the overall commander of the cavalry. Lucan could not understand Lord Raglan's request. Because the Balaklava Plain is shaped somewhat like an upside-down saucer, Lucan could not see what was

The original order that set the Light Brigade in motion, written down on Raglan's instruction by Richard Airey. Lord Lucan's misreading of the note led to the tragic Charge of the Light Brigade.

A. W. Kinglake, in The Invasion of the Crimea, *defends Captain Nolan against the charge of responsibility for the fatal charge of the Light Brigade.*

"Nolan was the last man in the whole army who would have been capable of sending our squadrons down the North Valley instead of to the line of the Heights; for, besides that he had come fresh from the high ground which commanded a full view of the enemy's position, and had just been gathering the true purpose of the orders from the lips of Lord Raglan himself; it so happened that he had a special and even personal interest in the recapture of the heights and the guns [which had been lost by the Turks in the first action of the day]."

plainly visible to Lord Raglan standing 350 feet above him. The only guns Lord Lucan could see were those located at the far end of the North Valley. After a curt exchange with Nolan, Lucan incorrectly concluded that it was these guns that Raglan wanted him to attack, and correctly surmised that an attack on those massed Russian guns would be sheer madness.

Now the tragedy unfolded. Lucan disliked and envied Nolan, who was a renowned expert horseman and the author of several important tracts on cavalry tactics. He did not press the matter, and remained perplexed by the order. As historian John Selby explains, "Sadly, Lucan's pride barred him from questioning Nolan further."[22]

Still confused by the instructions, Lord Lucan rode over to his hated brother-in-law and ordered Lord Cardigan to attack the guns. Cardigan too could not see what was plain to Lord Raglan. Cardigan, like Lucan, only knew about the powerful battery of Russian guns that guarded the far end of the North Valley.

Lucan told Cardigan to "advance steadily and keep your men well in hand." Cardigan responded, "Certainly, sir, but allow me to point out to you that the Russians have a battery in the valley in our front, and batteries and riflemen on each flank." To which Lucan responded, "I cannot help that. It is Lord Raglan's positive order that the Light Brigade attacks immediately."[23]

The Charge of the Light Brigade

Cardigan, like Lucan, did not attempt to clarify the situation with Nolan, the man who best knew Lord Raglan's mind at the moment. Nolan was Cardigan's inferior and far better respected among the soldiers. Lord Cardigan was an intensely jealous man.

Instead, Cardigan decided to carry out Raglan's order in every detail. He lined up

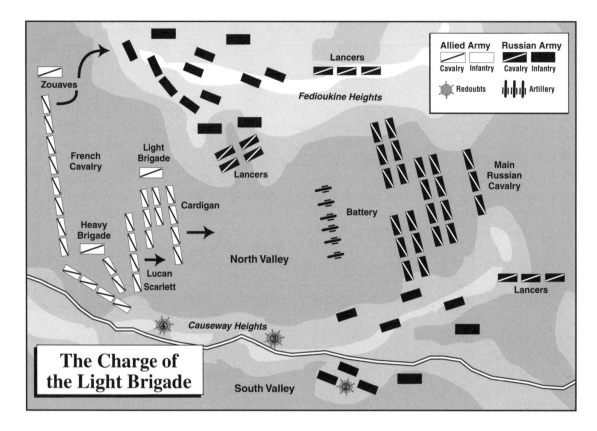

the Light Brigade, 673 gallant troopers, and then rode off at their head, down the "valley of Death," leading them to glory and to destruction.

At the very last moment Nolan realized that a horrible misunderstanding had taken place. Breaking out of battle formation, he waved his arm in Cardigan's direction in an attempt to turn Cardigan's charge to the right. He never delivered his warning. Captain Nolan was the first person to die by an enemy bullet during the deadly and unnecessary action.

The doomed Light Brigade rode down the valley, fired on by Russian gunners atop the Fedioukine Heights to their left and the Russian gunners manning the captured British guns on the Causeway Heights. Those who made it through the deadly gauntlet crashed into the Russian battery at the far end of the valley with such force that they actually overran the battery and spiked some of the Russian guns.

Any damage they inflicted came at a terrible price. Dead and dying horses littered the valley floor; scores more died on the return ride up the valley back to their starting position. Their way back was eased only by the fact that French Zouaves had by then overwhelmed the guns on the Fedioukine Heights.

The Heavy Brigade, waiting partway down the valley to receive the survivors, tried to "cover the retreat of the miserable remnants of that band of heroes as they returned to the place they had so late quitted in all the pride of life." [24]

Of the 673 men who charged out that late October morning, only 192 were fit for service at roll call that afternoon. Miraculously, Lord Cardigan, riding his charger Ronald, rode through the Russian battery, turned, and made the return trip up the valley unscathed.

Cardigan did not stop to assist or inquire after the well-being of his men. To his mind that was not the task of a proper British officer. Officers led, soldiers followed. His only emotion was fury at the fallen Captain Nolan, who had tried to ride across Cardigan's path at the beginning of the charge when Nolan realized that Cardigan was heading in the wrong direction.

When Lord Raglan rode up to demand an explanation, Cardigan demonstrated no remorse. Loudly he proclaimed that he was only following Lucan's direction. And with that, Lord Cardigan went off to relax aboard his yacht while the cries of terribly mauled horses shot by harriers echoed behind him.

Consequences of the Battle

So ended the Battle of Balaklava. Lords Raglan, Lucan, and Cardigan's actions that day demonstrated that modern warfare called for the leadership of professionally trained soldiers, not high-born, haughty, and unskilled figureheads.

There were additional consequences. The discouraged British lost partial control of the approaches to the port of Balaklava because the Russians retained their

This depiction of the fated Charge of the Light Brigade shows the determined looks of the cavalry as they proceed toward what can only be called mass suicide.

An Act of Brutality

After the tragic charge, a few remaining British struggled up the valley in an effort to escape. Reporter William Howard Russell describes what happened in General Todleben's History of the Defence of Sebastopol.

"There took place an act of atrocity without parallel in the modern warfare of civilized nations. The Russian gunners, when the storm of cavalry passed, returned to their guns. They saw their own cavalry mingled with the troopers who had just ridden over them, and to the eternal disgrace of the Russian name, the miscreants poured a murderous volley of grape and canister on the mass of struggling men and horses, mingled friend and foe, in one common ruin. It was as much as our Heavy Cavalry Brigade could do to cover the retreat of the miserable remnants of that band of heroes as they returned to the place they had so late quitted in all the pride of life."

hold over three of the redoubts. Their cavalry was crippled. And the relative strength of the British army in the Crimea began to decline in terms of the increasing power of the French.

Times reporter William Howard Russell wrote a moving letter, more of praise than condemnation, to his newspaper in the aftermath of the charge:

> If the exhibition of the most brilliant values, of the excess of courage, and of a daring which would have reflected luster on the best days of chivalry can afford full consolation for the disaster of today, we can have no reason to regret the melancholy loss which we sustained in a contest with a savage and barbarian enemy.[25]

The tribute could not conceal the fact that prospects for an immediate victory over the Russians remained as elusive as ever.

For the Russians, the situation now looked more promising. Although the Russians had suffered several setbacks, they won the last action of the battle. Gleefully their leaders displayed their trophies, banners from the redoubts and the British guns, before the inhabitants and defenders of Sebastopol. To the Russians the guns signaled ultimate victory over the British. Menshikov concluded that the British were far weaker than he expected. And so he decided to undertake a still larger military action to try to drive them out of the Crimea before the onset of the terrible Russian winter.

Chapter

5 The Battle of Inkerman

In the Inkerman action, whole regiments melted, losing a fourth of their men, while they were coming into musket range.

—Russian infantry officer

A brief calm followed the dramatic events of the Battle of Balaklava as both sides regrouped and assessed their damages. The Russians and the British each had to decide if the disadvantages of withdrawal outweighed the disadvantages of prolonging the war. Important issues, including the growing casualty counts and the lateness of the fighting season, had to be considered. Even a temporary halt to the fighting meant the armies would immediately begin preparations to go into winter quarters.

British Assessment of Its Position

The British high command concluded that its army more or less held its own on October 25, 1854. However, with the loss of the Light Brigade, the British would now have to maintain their position with only half their previous cavalry strength. British soldiers continued to die at an alarming rate. In addition, the British faced a major logistical problem: The Russians controlled the Woronzov Road. This important artery ran across the Causeway Heights from Sebastopol in the west to Yalta in the east. Russian control of the road meant that the

British soldiers pick up the dead, dying, and wounded after the Battle of Balaklava. The British lost half of their cavalry strength during the effort.

British were restricted to the use of a narrow, unpaved path as they moved supplies from Balaklava to the army in the hills six miles distant. What effect the impending rainy season would have on their transportation problems remained to be seen.

Finally, a major political concern loomed over the British high command and influenced the decision to remain. The problem was the French. The British were uncomfortable with the alliance. Trust had not developed between the two armies and a lingering fear remained among many Englishmen, both in the Crimea and back home, that in the not too distant future the French emperor would launch an attack against Britain.

Until now, British forces had sustained the main brunt of Russian attacks. If the allies stayed much longer in the Crimea, attrition alone would necessarily force the British army into a subordinate role; the British had no ready reserves to send to Raglan, and feared the French would see British military weakness as an opportunity to strike. The French, on the other hand, were largely unscathed, and yet Napoleon continued to send large numbers of reinforcements until the French army of sixty thousand men dwarfed the tiny British army. So the British decided to fight one more battle against the Russians. They hoped it would be their last in the Crimea.

The British planned their attack for November 7, 1854. British soldiers openly stacked scaling ladders at the Balaklava quay in preparation for use against Russian fortifications. The significance of the ladders was apparent to everyone, including Russian spies. But before the British could attack, the Russians upset their plans.

A Russian Ultimatum

Meanwhile, the Russians rejoiced over the results of the Battle of Balaklava. Their booty—the captured Turkish banners and British field guns—meant that the Russians had wounded the enemy. Perhaps these trophies of war portended an eventual Russian victory over the invaders of the Crimea.

Back in St. Petersburg, however, Tsar Nicholas was not pleased with the performance of his army. He demanded that Menshikov immediately provide him with an unambiguous victory. To that end Nicholas sent his third and fourth sons, the Grand Dukes Nicholas and Michael, to observe events and report their findings to their father. The implication was clear: If Menshikov failed, he would be replaced

Tsar Nicholas I (pictured) was not pleased with the Russian army's performance at Balaklava and threatened Menshikov with dismissal if he did not end the conflict quickly.

with a general who could drive the British, French, and Turkish soldiers out of the Crimean peninsula.

Clearly, each side had determined to go on the offensive once more before the onset of winter. Raglan wanted victory over the Russians before the French gained all the glory. Nicholas forced a battle on his army in order to restore the honor of Russia. The result of making military decisions within a political context was the bloodbath known to history as the Battle of Inkerman.

Menshikov's Plan

The British Second Division thinly manned Cossack Mountain, a high place overlooking the port of Sebastopol where the deserted town of Inkerman lay in ruins. The troops on the promontory were somewhat isolated from the other British divisions because of the roughness of the terrain and the lack of efficient communications. In addition, their position was precarious because their right flank had no protection except for the ruggedness of the terrain. They also were very much isolated from the French army, whose encampments were several miles to the southwest. British vulnerability seemed to provide a Russian opportunity.

Aleksandr Menshikov planned his attack on the British at Inkerman for the early morning hours of November 5. He counted on the element of surprise; his soldiers were to overrun the British in their advance positions at a weak, minimally fortified redoubt called Shell Hill and then drive them from their center of command at another weak redoubt called Home Ridge.

In a reckless decision, Tsar Nicholas ordered forced marches of additional assault troops from Bessarabia, a district that lies between Russia and modern-day Rumania, to the Crimea. The exertion cost many lives along the way. The exhausted, demoralized soldiers from Bessarabia and their commanding generals arrived at Sebastopol only the evening before the Battle of Inkerman.

With the addition of the Bessarabian army, Menshikov had at his disposal between 100,000 and 120,000 men. This force far more than doubled the total number of allied troops in the Crimea. Menshikov determined to commit 60,000 of these soldiers to battle on November 5. He provided his forces with 234 field guns, large reserves, and the promise of naval bombardment from two Russian warships offshore.

According to Menshikov's plan, Generals Paul Gorchakov and Pavel Liprandi would attack from the east and General F. F. von Moller would command the center of the Russian forces. General P. A. Dannenberg, Menshikov's second in command, directed the overall operation. Menshikov himself decided to watch the entire battle in the company of the tsar's two sons.

An essential part of Menshikov's plan called for the attack to begin before dawn on the morning of November 5. The troops would rely on the cover of darkness as well as the heavy fog that often covered the hills to screen their climb up the steep ridges of Cossack Mountain to the Inkerman battleground.

Menshikov also sent several small detachments of soldiers out of the port of Sebastopol in the direction of the two major French encampments. He intended this deployment of Russian troops near the

French lines to contain the French in their campsites when word reached them that a major battle was under way.

The Russian attack began as planned. Early Sunday morning the ringing of church bells helped to muffle the sounds of the huge army straining to climb the hills in stealth. The Russians had tied pieces of cloth around clanking pieces of gear, and rainfall and fog made all sights and sounds indistinct that day.

Luck also played a major role in easing the Russian climb to the top of Cossack Mountain: The British high command chose to ignore all rumors of an impending attack.

It is a curious fact of historic interest that some British soldiers even received letters from their families in England warning them that a Russian attack was imminent. But again, Lord Raglan did not employ spies and dismissed unofficial sources of information, even when the information came from the families of soldiers in England who had read it in their own newspapers.

So the British army remained unprepared for the approaching mass of Russian soldiers, who were themselves not an eager lot. The darkness, rain, and fog that hid them from the British also obscured their own way on the dangerous climb.

The conditions that facilitated the initial surprise now worked against the Russians and in favor of the defenders. The fog and the rain that concealed the climb of the soldiers now made it difficult for their officers to see the battlefield clearly. Menshikov's plan of attack required a great deal of coordination among the different units. But hills and ravines separated the various Russian commanders from one another and confused their lo-

Lord Raglan was unprepared for the massive Russian attack against his forces, despite having heard many rumors of the action, even from the British home front.

cations. Moreover, Menshikov had not briefed his staff competently; they found it difficult to execute orders they did not understand. Still worse, two of the generals had arrived from Bessarabia only the night before and they knew little of the terrain they had to capture.

First Contact

Still the battle had to be fought. Once the heights had been scaled the Russian troops arranged themselves into their customary massed column formations. They began to move toward their first objective, Shell Hill, and the line of pickets who guarded the approaches to this modest fortified position. The soldiers plodded along, working their way through thick underbrush and around stands of trees. They had a terrible time disentangling their field artillery pieces from underbrush. In the heavy fog it was difficult for the troops to tell enemy soldiers from bushes, which took on menacingly distorted forms in the darkness.

Soon the Russians encountered a thin line of British pickets, some of them asleep, most half frozen, who had taken up their positions in front of Shell Hill. The pickets were caught unawares. Tsarist Russian military engineer Edward Todleben describes the pitiful condition of these British troops: "Their outposts, soaked in rain, shivered on the cold blast of an icy wind, and half stupid with fatigue and lack of motion, did not lend much attention to what passed in our camp."[26] But before they were completely surrounded they managed to fire their rifles to warn the sleeping British camp that it was under attack.

One British cavalry officer, attached to the First Division, corroborates the surprise of the attack in a notation he entered in his diary the next day:

> Under cover of a thick mist and fog the Russians attacked our pickets in front of the First Division and in part all along the line. We turned out without any breakfast and remained sitting on our horses til about twelve thirty.[27]

"Like Fighting in a Nightmare"

At first Lord Raglan believed that the Russian attack represented only a small probing action. But very soon Raglan and his division commanders realized their error. They pieced together enough information to perceive the size and the nature of the menace they faced. The Russian attack near Inkerman was a major assault, closing in on the British from several directions simultaneously. And apparently the Russians had enormous reserves of manpower upon which they could draw.

The battle, or rather the series of violent clashes that began before dawn and lasted well into the afternoon, eight hours later, was like no other battle of the war. Neither commanding general played a role in the battle. Strictly speaking, there was no battle line to command.

Instead a large number of short, fierce encounters took place between huge units of poorly armed Russians and small units of well-armed British soldiers. The British units acted throughout the day as independent forces under their immediate commanding officers.

Unable to fight the British in fixed positions, the usual Russian battle tactics failed. The size of units meant very little in the surreal atmosphere atop Cossack Mountain that day. Instead the Russians stumbled into one another in the dark and then the fog. Their cavalry and mobile batteries were for the most part useless in the thick underbrush of the mountain.

The battlefield indeed was a very confused place. Historian Christopher Hibbert reports that

> Men looked like bushes, bushes like men. On both sides they were wearing overcoats and it was almost impossible to tell who were friends and who were enemies. It was like fighting in a nightmare, only the fear was real and so was the pain.[28]

Masses of British and Russian troops fight in a lethal frenzy of hand-to-hand combat during the Battle of Inkerman.

If the Russians' confidence was based on strength in numbers that day, the British drew additional strength from the knowledge that they were fighting a last-stand battle. Officers fought alongside their men in frantic engagements. General Sir John Pennefather led his men into numerous actions and had two horses shot dead from under him. In another engagement Sir George Cathcart was shot through the heart and died instantaneously. The queen's cousin, George, duke of Cambridge, also had his horse killed under him during the height of the battle.

The story of the British general Strangeways is particularly poignant. The old artillery general, a veteran of the Battle of Waterloo, mortally wounded from a burst of shell, is said to have asked his companions, "Will someone kindly assist me off my horse? I want to be taken away to die among my gunners."[29]

On the battlefield soldiers appeared as ghosts, emerging momentarily from the mist to defend a position and then disappearing just as suddenly. During a momentary lifting of the fog British sharpshooters managed to identify and kill the Russian

general F. I. Soimonov, his two deputies, and an artillery commander. The only impressions many of the survivors of the battle remembered about the day were the constant shouts of men in the heat of combat, killing the enemy, and trying to contact members of their units.

The killing took on a savage aspect as hand-to-hand combat forced the soldiers to see the faces of the enemy. Many Russians, too intoxicated to fight because the officers had given them too much vodka to quell their battlefield jitters, crawled into the bushes to hide. According to Hibbert:

Many of them had been sent out that morning with extra rations of vodka and brandy and some of them were drunk, but their fear had not been dulled. Finding themselves alone, no longer part of the encouraging and comforting mass in which they had been training to fight, they began to lose their nerve. They hid in the bushes or lay down where they were, pretending to be dead. Sensing their fear, the English soldiers rushed at them like wolves, jabbing furiously with their bayonets at the long grey coats or swinging their rifles around by the barrels to bring the heavy stock down with a sickly, satisfying thud against the white, strangely expressionless faces.[30]

There also were numerous reports of Russian soldiers coming upon British wounded and stabbing them with their bayonets where they lay.

The minié rifle proved itself that day. Huge numbers of charging Russian troops fell under the impact of the precise firing of the British long before the less-efficient Russian guns could be aimed and fired.

The French Join the Battle

The French eventually realized that the Russian move against their position was a feint designed to keep them out of the battle. About ten in the morning, five hours after the fighting began, the French sent troops to Cossack Mountain.

British pride prevented Lord Raglan from admitting that he needed French assistance. Nevertheless, the arrival of thirteen thousand French soldiers saved the British army. By eleven in the morning already one-third of the five thousand British defenders were dead or wounded and the outnumbered rest were exhausted by the battle.

The French fought fiercely against the Russians and their plentiful reserves persuaded General Dannenberg to consider pulling back his forces. Meanwhile, Menshikov remained reluctant to throw his own thousands of reserves into the battle. Finally, the Russian artillery officers realized that their cannons were having little effect and began to withdraw them.

A British Soldier's Experience of Battle

Captain John Elton of the 55th Regiment wrote a letter describing for his family his experiences during the Battle of Inkerman. The letter is quoted by Christopher Hibbert in The Destruction of Lord Raglan.

"There was nothing to be done but push to the front and I soon joined the advanced picket which I found in much the same state with regard to the arms as my own. We retired gradually before them as they were coming on in masses of columns supported with a very powerful artillery, and soon had more desperate work. Almost hand to hand in thick brushwood with the guns playing on us in a most fearful way, and our answering them over our heads, while we were firing musketry into each other at fifteen and twenty paces distant, now and then charging and driving them back with the bayonet and then being driven back by superior numbers again."

Russian Withdrawal

Seeing the withdrawal of the cannons, General Dannenberg lost all enthusiasm for the awful battle and began to pull back his men. The Russians began the difficult descent of the mountain; Menshikov and the grand dukes continued to sit where they had sat all day, about a half mile from Dannenberg's position on Shell Hill.

By five o'clock in the afternoon the ground around Inkerman was covered with bodies, many French and British but mostly Russian. Around the areas repeatedly attacked, captured, defended, and attacked again—the Sandbag Battery, Shell Hill, and the Barrier—the dead and dying lay many layers deep, presenting truly ghastly scenes of incredible slaughter. In all, about eleven thousand Russians lay dead or wounded that day. Six hun-

Allied and Russian troops face off as the Battle of Inkerman wears on, littering the battlefield with bodies.

The French Zouave units advance to aid the British troops during the Battle of Inkerman. The Russians then retreated, and the battle ultimately resulted in a stalemate.

dred British were killed and two thousand more wounded along with several hundred French casualties.

Results of the Battle

At the end of the battle, the entire Inkerman ridge still remained in the hands of the allies. Lord Raglan wanted to pursue the Russians back down the mountain. The French general, Canrobert, refused to join him and so Raglan, as he had done at the Alma, abandoned the idea.

The grand dukes wrote home to their father, Tsar Nicholas, that Menshikov was incompetent and had failed to use his troops properly. They believed that the Russians would have been victorious at Inkerman if only Menshikov had thrown the Russian reserves into action at a critical moment in the fight. The tsar eventually replaced Menshikov with General Gorchakov.

In the end, the killing accomplished nothing. The battle was indecisive. The allies

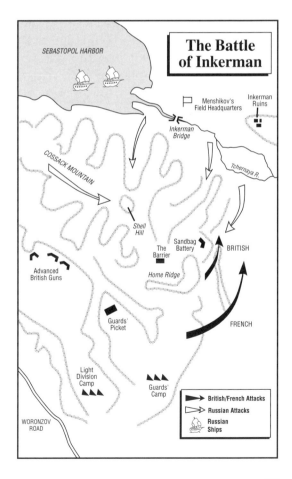

A Son Writes to His Father About Inkerman

Alexander Gordon, son of the British prime minister, wrote to his father about his experiences in the Battle of Inkerman. Gordon's quote is taken from Alan Palmer's The Banner of Battle.

"You will have heard that we have had another terrible battle in which we were at length victorious but with a loss which we can ill afford. Owing to the mercy of God, I again escaped unhurt, although my horse was shot under me. The battle lasted nine hours and hard fighting most of it. You need not expect to hear of the fall of Sebastopol this winter, the utmost we can do is to protect ourselves in our present positions and shall be very fortunate if we succeed in that."

demonstrated that the Russian army, despite its enormous size, could not push the British and French into the sea. On the other hand, seasoned British troops needed for an attack on the port of Sebastopol died at Inkerman or sustained wounds that eventually proved fatal.

It now was quite clear that the allies could not mount an attack against the Russian port because of their inadequate manpower and supplies. A stalemate existed; they were stuck in the Crimea. Thus, while the Russian army settled in to spend its winter within the city and port of Sebastopol, the allied army, particularly the remnants of the once-glorious British army, settled in for the horrors of a winter encampment in a remote corner of the world without protection against the elements.

6 Life in the War Zone

But the light of her lamp shone beyond the tragic beds of the Barrack Hospital and pierced the conscience of the British public so that they, and not the patient soldiers, rose up at last against the monstrous callousness of the authorities.

—Cecil Woodham-Smith,
Florence Nightingale

The common soldier of the nineteenth century lived a precarious existence. Often he was treated badly by superior officers who put the welfare of their horses above that of the men whom they commanded. The soldier suffered from insufficient rations and a nutrient-deficient diet. Of course, periodically the enemy threatened the soldier's life. His most lethal enemies, however, were disease and the inability of all combatants' medical corps to treat the sick and wounded with the proper care.

The Crimean War was an extraordinarily costly war in terms of loss of life. In this regard it may be classed with the wars of earlier centuries, in which the weapons of the enemy were not the primary killers of soldiers, rather than the wars of the twentieth century, in which the technological ingenuity of the enemy could destroy an entire army in a single action.

The vast majority of the British troops who went to the Crimea in 1854 did not return. They were destroyed not by the Russian enemy but by far more deadly foes—neglect, disease, filth, ignorance, arrogance, and stupidity. These evils were not new—armies throughout history had perished anonymously and at the hands of the same killers, considered the price a nation paid to engage in foreign wars. The dead were forgotten by all but the families who privately mourned the loss of their loved ones.

But that this dreadful state of affairs continued throughout the nineteenth century, in supposedly advanced societies, was particularly appalling. The leaders of Russia and Turkey, for example, had neither the money, administrative systems, or medical knowledge to care for their soldiers in the field. In fact, the concept that soldiers warranted special attention did not exist. Thousands of others were available to replace those who died.

The French Advantage

Emperor Napoleon's army also suffered tragic losses due to disease and to the terrible climate of the Crimea. Because of their experiences during the Napoleonic Wars and later in North Africa, however, the French government understood, as others did not, the importance of adequate supplies of food and medical care. Thus, the French government did not disperse among multiple departments responsibility for supplying the army. Supply functions were closely controlled. This resulted in a commissary service far more organized and systematic in its approach to provisioning the French army than was the case for any other country in the 1850s. In general it can be said of the French army that its officers valued the services that the troops provided. They understood the importance of keeping the army in combat readiness. Although they suffered from the same horrors of disease that afflicted the British and Russian armies, the French army in the Crimea did not experience the kind of neglect and callous disregard for the lives of the troops that was the plight of the Russian, the Turkish, and even the British soldiers.

Disease: The Most Lethal Enemy

The catastrophe of disease added to the already dismal arrangements made for the troops. Particularly for the British the antiquated and inadequate medical system simply fell apart under the strain of caring for thousands of ill soldiers. At times more soldiers were in the hospitals than in the trenches.

The generals in charge blamed the numerous victims rather than their own inadequate arrangements for the hellish situation that prevailed. "The medical services would have been perfectly adequate," announced the London Hospital Report of 1855, "if it had not been for the casualties."[31]

The inadequacy of the system, already apparent at the camps at Varna, became a human catastrophe with the transport of casualties aboard "hospital ships" in the Crimea to the hospitals at Scutari, on the Bosporus. For the soldiers the trip itself was a nightmare. The hospital ships in fact were not equipped to handle the casualties. The men, some of them already dead, were brought aboard the ships, still wearing the clothing in which they had landed in the Crimea months before.

There were no doctors to attend to their wounds or even fresh water to slake their terrible thirst. Men with fresh ampu-

Wounded soldiers converse in a crude field hospital constructed on the front at Sebastopol. The unsanitary conditions in these hospitals often hastened the deaths of the wounded soldiers.

This illustration of the field hospital at Scutari does not reveal the notoriously poor conditions of the hospital. The hospital offered no running water or plumbing, and the corridors were filthy.

tations were thrown down on the decks beside men suffering from cholera and dysentery. Their vomit, blood, and body wastes mingled on the open decks on which they lay.

Then began the horrible sea journey of three hundred miles. Many men died en route from neglect and malnutrition. The hospital ships were more aptly called death ships; those who managed to survive the gruesome ordeal of the sea voyage faced the greater hell of the military facilities in Scutari.

That hell included the mass of flies, fleas, and rats that lived in the hospitals. Historian Hibbert describes the rats as "those great big grey fellows that scuttled and crawled over the moldering floors"[32] of the hospital.

British Hospitals

The British opened a second hospital, the Barracks, to deal with the overflow from their primary facility. Occasionally French soldiers arrived at these hospitals, but the French had more efficient field hospitals where many of their sick and wounded received care.

The British hospitals had little to recommend them as healing institutions. Even when the first contingent of sick soldiers arrived, the hospitals could not care for them adequately. They were old, ramshackle buildings, which the Turkish government previously had used to house soldiers. There was no clean running water or plumbing. There were no kitchen facilities for preparing wholesome food or sterile supplies to keep the sick and wounded warm and clean. An actual cesspool ran under the floor of the Barracks Hospital. The filth and disease it spread killed hundreds of patients before the source of the contamination was identified and removed.

Historian Palmer reports that

There were no tables, chairs, a shortage of doctors, a shortage of drugs, lamps and candles, as well as basic domestic furniture. The rain penetrated the rooms and on bad days caused the latrines to overflow and flood the floors. Sometimes when a gale swept down the Bosporus rickety windows would blow in on the sick and wounded as they struggled to survive. Surgeons carried out amputations without anaesthetic within the sight and sound of those next waiting attention, making the filthy corridors hideous.[33]

In December 1854 alone, two thousand British soldiers died in the Scutari hospitals of various causes.

The Role of the Press

Fortunately for the British soldier, England in the 1850s enjoyed the benefits of an uncensored and inexpensive press. By the end of 1854, it became increasingly difficult to conceal what the commanders in the field knew from the public at home. Every day the newspapers in London and elsewhere denounced the failure of the British government to ensure the well-being of its troops.

The newspapers demanded that drastic improvements take place in the medical and food provisioning of the army in the Crimea and that living accommodations improve substantially. If these changes did not take place, the newspapers warned, the army would cease to exist.

The *Times* of London led the way. Its editor, John Delane, traveled to the Crimea to investigate for himself the conditions under which the troops lived. He was enraged by the officers' callous disregard for the common soldier.

Upon his return to London, he began to publish the dispatches of William Howard Russell, the fiery, dark-bearded Irishman who served as the primary *Times* correspondent at the Crimean front. With eloquence and pathos Russell chronicled

William Russell of the Times *takes notes while on location in the Crimea. Journalists such as Russell brought the horrors of the Crimea back to the British home front.*

the troops' day-to-day suffering as a result of military and political mismanagement.

Pieces from Russell such as the following could not help to arouse public sentiment:

> Do not suffer our soldiers to be killed by antiquated imbecility. Do not hand them over to the mercies of ignorant etiquette and effete seniority, but give the sick every chance which skill, energy and abundance of the best medications can afford them. The heads of departments may rest assured that the country will grudge no expense on their part, nor any other connected with the interests and efficiency of the corps d'elite which England has sent from her shores.[34]

In case people continued to doubt the gravity of the situation, the newspapers provided pictorial evidence. For the first time numerous graphic photographs of the camps and the ragged conditions of the soldiers appeared in the newspapers. The public was enraged.

The Role of John Hall

Dr. John Hall received a commission to head the medical establishment in Turkey during the Crimean campaign. He was an influential physician who resented the fact that he had been sent to Turkey. Although Queen Victoria eventually honored Hall with the title of K.C.B. (Knight Commander of the Order of the Bath) for his services, his cynical critics said the title really meant "Knight of the Crimean Burial Grounds."[35]

More than the ever-increasing number of sick and wounded who demanded his attention, Hall bitterly resented outside interference in his work. When the British public learned how poorly the wounded were treated, several governmental investigative committees went to the Crimea to see for themselves how Hall provided medical care for soldiers. Public concern also led John Delane of the *Times* to help arrange for the collection of funds to relieve the troops' suffering.

It also inaugurated a crusade launched by the one true heroine of the Crimean War, Florence Nightingale. Outraged by the medical news from the Crimea and determined to demonstrate that female nurses could attend to soldiers in the field, she also wanted to destroy public prejudice against nurses and thereby make nursing a respectable profession for women in England.

Florence Nightingale

With the assistance of Sir Sidney Herbert, the secretary at war under the earl of Aberdeen (George Hamilton-Gordon), Nightingale proceeded to organize a group of forty nurses to go to the Crimea. Nightingale was in a unique position to take up her crusade. She was an unmarried upper-class Englishwoman with a spotless reputation. Against the protests of her family, Nightingale had received some training as a nurse in Europe. Even more unusual was the fact that at the time the war began she already directed a small medical clinic on Harley Street in the heart of London's medical district.

Herbert saw Nightingale as the perfect vehicle to bring comfort to the soldiers in

Florence Nightingale brought respectability to the profession of nursing during the Crimean War. Before Nightingale, nurses were thought to be no better than prostitutes.

the Crimea. He personally invited her to take up the challenge, supported by public demands that goods and funds immediately go to the Crimea to assist the ragged and suffering army. Viewed as incorruptible, Florence Nightingale was their choice to administer the money raised by the Fund for the Sick and Wounded sponsored by the *Times*.

The Arrival of British Nurses at Scutari

The nurses arrived in Scutari, just across the Bosporus from Constantinople, on November 4, 1854, the eve of the Battle of Inkerman. It had taken them two weeks to reach their destination. It had taken the British army four months. Nightingale carried the title of Superintendent of the Female Nursing Establishment on the English General Hospitals in Turkey. She quickly discovered how little that splendid title meant.

At the hospital at Scutari hundreds of casualties from the Alma and Balaklava were lying largely unattended in the filthy corridors of the old and decaying building. Historian Alan Palmer writes that the nurses found "lines of verminous beds [that] stretch down foul miles of corridors which the Hospital Commissioners later described as a sea of sewage." [36]

As she viewed this nightmare of human suffering, Miss Nightingale discovered that her main enemy was the medical establishment. John Hall had thus far reported that everything was under control. Now, backed by his subordinates, he resisted the help of the nurses and the goods that the money in their charge could purchase.

The Lady with the Lamp

Historian Alan Palmer, in The Banner of Battle, *quotes a description of Florence Nightingale that appeared in the* Times *of London in November 1854. It is that image that most frequently comes to mind when the name of Florence Nightingale is mentioned.*

"Whenever there is disease in its most dangerous form, and the hand of the spoiler distressingly night, there is this incomparable woman sure to be seen; her benignant presence is an influence of good comfort, even amidst the struggles of expiring nature. She is a 'ministering angel,' without any exaggeration, in these hospitals; and as her slender form glides quietly along each corridor, every poor fellow's face softens with gratitude at the sight of her. When all the medical officers have retired for the night, and silence and darkness have settled down upon those miles of prostrate sick, she may be observed alone, with a little lamp in her hand, making the solitary rounds."

Florence Nightingale (left) and fellow nurses aid the wounded at the hospital at Scutari. Note the clean conditions and open windows, both advocated by Nightingale.

Florence Nightingale continuously fought the medical establishment as well as the diseases that were killing off the army. She wrote to Sidney Herbert that she found herself surrounded by men who "are neither gentlemen, nor men of education nor even men of business but men whose only object is to keep themselves out of blame."[37]

They certainly had no understanding of the role the newly arrived nurses could play. Indeed, Nightingale came to realize that in the medical profession there was a belief "that it required nothing but a disappointment in love, or incapacity in other things, to turn a woman into a good nurse."[38]

Hall and his fellow doctors demonstrated the characteristic prejudice against women in positions of authority. They railed against the women's efforts to work in the hospital itself. They were outraged by their efforts to clean out the filth, to provide separate beds and linen to men who had been lying in their own filth for days, perhaps even weeks.

They even protested when the nurses cooked soft food for the sick soldiers to replace the indigestible hard biscuits and dried salted meat that were the staples of the British soldier's diet. The nurses had to convince the doctors that the soldiers' teeth had become loosened and their gums soft and spongy because of the scurvy rampant in the army by the end of 1854.

And so for weeks after their arrival, the nurses were not permitted to assist in the hospital while the wounded continued to suffer. It took the massive catastrophe at Inkerman to force the doctors to give in.

Nursing Experience

Elizabeth Davis was one of the nurses who worked at the General Hospital at Scutari. She graphically describes her experiences when finally she was able to attend to the inmates late in November:

> I began to open some of their wounds. The first that I touched was a case of frost bite. The toes of both the man's feet fell off with the bandages. The hands of another fell off at the wrist. It was a fortnight, or from that to six weeks, since the wounds of many of those men had been looked at and dressed. One soldier had been wounded at the Alma. . . . His wound had not been dressed for five weeks and I took at least a quart of maggots from it. From many of the other patients I removed them in handfuls.[39]

Every nurse had similar stories to relate. Florence Nightingale wrote in her letters that often all she could offer was the simple act of sitting beside a dying soldier, holding his hand in his last moments.

It would be many years before the British soldier in the field received the full and proper treatment he deserved from a respectful government. Yet Florence Nightingale and her nurses had begun a noble battle that ultimately proved successful. The British government expressed this hope in its reply to the report submitted to it by the Select Committee on the Army Before Sebastopol:

> Your Committee will now close their report, with a hope that every British army may in future display the great qualities which the noble army has displayed, and that none may hereafter be exposed to such suffering as are recorded in these pages.[40]

The work of Florence Nightingale and those who wished to reform the military medical and supply system did not help

A woman serves food to the troops of the Fourth Dragoons. Government and military officials both resisted allowing women to take action to improve conditions on the battlefields.

many of the soldiers of the Crimean War that first year. But over time tremendous strides were made on their behalf.

The Onset of Autumn

Unfortunately, the healthy soldiers were not much better off than the sick ones. The British soldiers suffered more than most. While the Russian army found some protection within the walls of Sebastopol and the French had received winter supplies, the British suffered from exposure and privation. The troops chopped down and burned every tree and every bush. When this fuel was exhausted, they hacked the roots of the trees from the nearly frozen ground to start pathetic little fires to warm their hands and to heat their water. Before long there was nothing left to burn.

The troops still wore the tatters of their summer uniforms long after the weather turned inclement. They stuffed these rags with straw and wrapped about their bodies whatever scraps of clothing they could improvise or take off the bodies of their dead comrades. Lieutenant William Richard wrote a letter describing the condition of the British army toward the end of 1854:

> The British officers wore beards so long that you could scarcely recognize even their faces. My own already is a foot long and in fact I look very much like an owl looking out of an ivy bush. I intend to turn all the hair to some good account if I return, the bed stuffing business.

Lieutenant Richard also provides a stark picture of the appearance of the clothing worn by some of the other officers and men:

Some of the officers had hay-bands bound around their legs, others had long stockings outside their rags of trousers; some had garters made from old knapsacks; others had leggings made from sheepskins, bullock hides, or horse hides—anything to keep out the extreme cold. Other men's coats were nothing but rags tacked together. As for head dress some had mess tin covers that could be pulled down well over the ears; others had coverings for the head made out of old blankets four or five times doubled. Some of their beards and moustaches were almost two inches long and some times these were so frozen that they could not open their mouths until they could get a fire to thaw them.[41]

Privation of Russian Soldiers

Russian soldiers during the Crimean War were even more deprived of necessities than were their British counterparts, according to historian Alexis S. Troubetzkoy in The Road to Balaklava.

"Russian soldiers were expected to make their own shirts, boots and underwear. The government supplied the materials. Regulation uniforms were to last two years, overcoats three years, belts, helmets and knapsacks ten years.

The officers were either nobles of hereditary families or nobles of lesser status. Only ten percent of these officers graduated from university or had received higher education in special cadet schools. Most of them barely had a minimal formal education and many were barely literate.

There were gross abuses in the army. Yet, despite the brutal treatment and privation of all sorts, the Russian Army developed a strong esprit de corps."

The horses, too, suffered horribly. By the end of November many had died of exposure and exhaustion. The few remaining scrawny animals painfully and slowly hauled goods up from the harbor. There was never enough food to feed them adequately.

When they were lucky, the troops' rations consisted of hard biscuits and salted meat. Like the afflicted hospital patients, those with scurvy could not chew such food. So men and animals grew weaker and waited hopefully for the order to withdraw into winter quarters. The order never came.

The Hurricane of the Century

Instead, they were subjected to nature's wrath: On the night of November 13, a storm called by observers the hurricane of the century struck the Crimean peninsula.

Already terribly cold in the days following the Battle of Inkerman on November 5, the wind began to blow furiously across the Crimea on November 13, striking the unprotected British camps positioned on the hills above Sebastopol. While the Russians huddled in stone houses in Sebastopol and the French crept into their prepared huts, the British army suffered. Historian Christopher Hibbert provides a graphic description of what the British soldiers experienced on November 13–14:

All morning the torrent raged and the rain blew down through the howling wind, and then at two o'clock the force of it slackened. Men got up from their hiding-places, covered in mud, their eyes streaming from the cold of the sleet, and looked at each other in a sort of despair, shivering in wet rags. The mud-covered ground was littered with the damp, sprawling canvas of the tents, broken lengths of rope, smashed boxes, torn blankets, furniture, pots; and against the windward side of the walls and protecting banks muddled piles of unrecognizable and mud slashed debris. The dead lay around the collapsed and tattered hospital tents and under the water logged canvas. Horses blown from their picket-ropes walked amidst the chaos and nibbled at the wet and sprawling bales of hay.[42]

A survivor of this first major blast of the Russian winter recalls that on November 13, "The state of our camp is beyond anything beastly. The mud is a foot deep all around the horses. The rain beats into our tents. How man or horse can stand this work much longer I know not."[43]

The storm, he continues, raged on the next day: "It blew fearfully, and the snow and sleet came down in showers. Everything that could be blown away was blown away. The miserable horses got nothing all day. Nothing could be gotten for them or given to them if got."[44]

Tragedy in the harbor matched the tragedy at the encampments. Several British vessels were destroyed when the winds crashed them against the rocks. The greatest loss, perhaps, was that of the *Prince*. The ship broke apart on the rocks on the anchorage of the outer harbor. In addition to the loss of the entire crew, the *Prince* went down with a cargo of forty thousand greatcoats and many thousands of boots, altogether an estimated five hundred tons of warm clothing. Had these items been

British soldiers shiver in the cold in their thin clothes and uninsulated tents. Many of the men died from exposure during the miserable winter of 1854–1855.

distributed, the troops would have been much better prepared to withstand the harsh weather.

Storms raged again on November 24 and 25. On November 25, William Howard Russell reported the following details in a letter to the *Times*:

> It is now pouring rain—the skies are black as ink—the wind is blowing over the staggering tents—the trenches are turned into dikes—in the tents the water is sometimes a foot deep—our men have neither warm nor waterproof clothing—and they are out for twelve hours at a time in the trenches—they are plunged into the inevitable miseries of a winter campaign—and not a soul seems to care for their comfort or even for their lives.[45]

The Russians were the only ones to benefit from the horrors visited on the British army. The Russians left the safety of Sebastopol and crept out to the trenches above Sebastopol where they frequently found British soldiers asleep or already dead from fatigue and exposure. Those asleep they bayoneted. Despite their fear of these Russian raids, the soldiers, overworked and half starved, fell asleep anyway and fell victim to the bayonets of the Russians.

A cavalry officer surveyed the situation in a letter to his family in England:

> We are as far from taking Sebastopol as we were two months ago, indeed I think further from it. Lord Raglan deserves no credit for the conduct of the campaign, and as to his staff, they are

The Balaklava harbor (pictured) was eventually linked to the allied camps by rail, which expedited supply delivery considerably.

abominable. Nothing can be worse. He abuses the cavalry, and blames us for the state they are in, when it is all his fault. God grant that I may return home once more, and spend the rest of my days in peace.[46]

The *Times* collected many of these letters and published them along with Russell's accounts. There were accusations that the *Times* was magnifying and sensationalizing the suffering of the troops, but when the *Morning Herald*, the *Manchester Guardian*, and the *Daily News* published similar accounts, they could not be ignored.

The stories, letters, and photographs were damning evidence. The public's reaction stirred the government from its stupor. Ships began to reach the near-frozen troops, laden with "flannel shirts, sheepskin coats, knitted hats, but especially with beer, sweets, biscuits and other forgotten luxuries."[47]

Slowly, the efforts of Florence Nightingale and her nurses began to reduce the army's mortality rate. The government began construction of a single-track military railroad from the port of Balaklava up to the highlands. Railroad construction went slowly, but every foot completed meant one less step taken by exhausted men and animals to get supplies to the men in the camps.

Improvements in Diet

Spring of 1855 brought the first British army kitchens to the Crimea. Alexis Soyer, the head chef of the Reform Club in London, arrived in the Crimea to volunteer his services. The Frenchman came armed with the full authority of Lord Panmure, the secretary of war who replaced Sidney Herbert. Soyer proceeded to attack the kitchens in the hospitals at Scutari and what passed for kitchens in the encampments above Sebastopol.

Soyer developed recipes for taking traditional army rations and turning them into nutritious soups and stews. He designed special utensils and equipment for cooking huge quantities of hot, tasty food at one time. Soyer also insisted that troops

Improvement in British Food Supplies

Cecil Woodham-Smith, in Florence Nightingale, *describes the efforts made by the chef Alexis Soyer to improve the food available to the British army. Soyer developed recipes using traditional army rations and turning them into nutritious meals. Woodham-Smith quotes from* Soyer's Culinary Campaign, *which appeared in 1857.*

"Stew:

Cut up or chop 50 lbs. of fresh beef in pieces of about 1/4 lb. each; put in the boiler, with 10 tablespoons of salt, two ditto of pepper, four ditto of sugar, onions 7 lbs. cut in slices; light the fire now, and then stir the meat with a spatula, let it stew from 20 to 30 minutes, or till it forms a thick gravy, then add a pound and a half of flour; mix well together, put in the boiler 18 quarts of water, stir well for a minute or two, regulate the stove to a moderate heat, and let simmer for about two hours. Mutton, pork or veal, can be stewed in a similar manner but will take a half hour less cooking. Note: A pound of rice may be added with greater advantage, ditto plain dumplings, ditto potatoes, as well as mixed vegetables."

The title page to Alexis Soyer's A Culinary Campaign. *Soyer took charge of the feeding of the British soldiers during the Crimean War.*

be permanently attached to the kitchens and taught how to cook and to bake bread and biscuits. Soyer also developed what he called the Scutari teapot, an invention capable of brewing up to fifty cups of tea at a time.

The changes Soyer brought about influenced British field, hospital, and ship kitchens for the next fifty years. Some of his recipes have survived in a book called *Soyer's Culinary Campaign,* which was published in 1857.

Thus, by the spring of 1855, long past the time when the original British army in the Crimea could benefit, the situation in the Crimea improved. England even began to bring in fresh recruits from England and India. Just in time, as it turned out, because the allies were about to renew their assault on Sebastopol.

7 The Siege of Sebastopol

*Hurray for the Crimea! Take Sebastopol in
a week or two and then into winter quarters.*

—Coronet Fischer,
in Anglesey, *'Little Hodge'*

The dramatic but brief battles of the early
Crimean War—Alma, Balaklava, Inkerman—
were secondary to the primary objective—
the destruction of Sebastopol. The siege of
the giant Russian naval base continued its
slow, painful, inefficient course over a period of nearly two years. The siege lasted
throughout the war and during the battles
of Inkerman and Balaklava, and although
devoting resources to the siege and attack
of Sebastopol might have ended the war
much earlier, it did not happen.

The siege should not have been difficult: Only a few Russian sailors and the
town's civilian population were left to defend the port. Menshikov's army had with-
drawn into the interior of the Crimean
peninsula. Only the Star Fort to the north
of the city, with a mere twelve of its forty-
seven guns facing the land approaches to
Sebastopol, separated the invading army
from its objective.

Thus, the port and city lay open for the
taking. It was virtually defenseless. Menshikov's desertion of the city and its arsenal made it possible for the allies to
achieve their stated objectives. They could

immediately attack, take the port, destroy
its ability to serve as a threat to Turkey, end
the war quickly, and go home.

Flank March Around Sebastopol

Instead General Saint-Arnaud decided
that the entire allied strategy to date had
been a mistake. He told Lord Raglan that
Sebastopol should not be attacked from
the north. Instead, the entire allied army
should march around Sebastopol and attack from the south.

The plan made no sense. For one
thing, no one in command knew what the
armies would encounter on the southern
side of the port. In addition, by marching around the town, the British and
French would march in long, undefended
lines through uncharted, woody terrain.
These lines would be easy to attack, especially since the allies would be marching
far inland, out of reach of the powerful
British fleet.

Lord Raglan wanted to attack Sebastopol immediately, but he listened to
Saint-Arnaud because he needed the support of the French army. Reluctantly he
agreed to attack the Russian port from its

southern side. And so began the thirty-hour-long flank march around undefended Sebastopol.

This unnecessary maneuver was responsible for the war dragging on for another eighteen months. It also led to the virtual destruction of the entire British army. In fact, hundreds of thousands of people would die before the war ended. Historian Cecil Woodham-Smith condemned the allied decision in very strong words:

> That week between 21st and 28th of September decided the fate of the British army. The obvious plan was to attack the northern side of Sebastopol, the side nearest to the Alma. But the French had doubts; there was no important fort on the northern side; the fortifications would prove too strong. The Allied commanders had set up no intelligence service whatsoever, and they were unaware that the fortifications were in bad repair and undermanned and that Prince Menshikov had withdrawn the army which had been allowed to escape after the Alma to the south side of the city. The Allies could have walked into Sebastopol [from the] north almost without firing a shot.[48]

Settling In

The allied leaders settled themselves in their respective ports, unloading supplies from their ships including a complete siege train. A siege train consists of a series of wagons pulled by horses, filled with artillery pieces, ammunition, wood, and other items necessary to initiate a siege and maintain a siege. When the British de-

cided on Balaklava as their port on September 25, British sailors began unloading this equipment. Then the equipment was hauled to the high ground overlooking Sebastopol and the artillery arranged to maximize the damage that could be done to the fortifications. The actual attack on the south side of the Russian naval base of Sebastopol did not begin until October 17, during which time Todleben had time to develop his own defensive system.

The aged John Bourgoyne, a siege expert from the Napoleonic Wars, directed the siege operations. British general Sir George Cathcart, who led the Fourth Division, was outraged by the delay caused by preparations for a siege. He referred to the Russian defense as little more than a "thing like a low park wall" and urged Raglan to attack immediately. "Land the siege trains!" Cathcart exploded. "But my dear Lord Raglan, what the devil is there to knock down?"[49]

Raglan did not heed the advice of some of his officers. He paid scant attention to the fact that the southern side of the town was about as poorly defended as the northern side. Immediate action meant almost certain victory. Instead, laboriously, the British dragged the siege train up from the ships, along with a large number of naval guns that they intended to use in their planned massive assault on the arsenal.

Russian Preparations

While the British plodded along with their siege plans, the Russians within Sebastopol used every available moment to create a defense. Colonel Edward Todleben, one of

The allied encampment on the plain before the Battle of Sebastopol. As the allies waited, Edward Todleben spent his time reinforcing Sebastopol to withstand a siege.

the greatest military engineers of the nineteenth century, led the defensive plan.

Todleben faced a daunting situation. The six major Russian fortifications lay in a semicircle of ruins with some smaller ones among them. East to west the major fortifications were called the Little Redan, the Malakoff Bastion, the Redan Bastion, the Flagstaff Bastion, the Central Bastion, and the Quarantine Bastion. In addition, some other defensive places, the Bastion du Mat, the Mamelon Bastion, and Fort Constantine, also urgently required repairs in order to form solid lines of defenses around the north and south sides of Sebastopol.

These fortifications had long ago ceased to be of great defensive value. They had been left to decay and needed considerable repair if they were to defend Sebastopol against the British, French, and Turks. Todleben himself feared allied attack. But, as reporter and historian William Howard Russell writes, the Russians

with joy inexpressible saw one fine morning long lines of earth which unmistakably revealed the purpose of the Allies. They were going to besiege Sebastopol. Here indeed was hope of safety, nay more, a guarantee of success. All in Sebastopol congratulated each other on this circumstance; all saw in it an important guarantee that the town might yet be saved.[50]

Todleben organized the Russians in Sebastopol to defend themselves. He organized squads of sailors from the port and citizens from the town, men, women, children, and even priests who assisted by walking through the crowds of workers, blessing them, their fortifications, and their tools. All kinds of people worked together on the dilapidated fortifications. Night and day they struggled to reinforce collapsed walls. They stocked the arsenals of the individual forts. They built a series of connecting tunnels among the forts so that defenders could move unexposed from one to the other. Then, by careful arrangement of guns, Todleben made it possible for one restored fort to assist the others by having its fields of fire overlap the others.

Allied soldiers like George Palmer Evelyn looked helplessly on as the work of reconstruction continued on the Russian side:

> We could see their workmen in the thousands, quite exposed and apparently much at their ease, as if engaged in some peaceful occupation. We left them unmolested. Shells thrown from two or three heavy mortars might have impeded them greatly—perhaps even obliged them to confine their work to the hours of night. But such a measure would not have been in character with the sublime repose which characterizes all our proceedings.[51]

The First Bombardment

Finally, on October 17, 1854, more than a month after their landing, the allies began

---

Russians Defend Sebastopol

Historian Christopher Hibbert, in The Destruction of Lord Raglan, *praises the work of Vice Admiral Kornilov, who took over the defense of Sebastopol when Menshikov deserted the port in September 1854.*

"When Menshikov deserted Sebastopol, Kornilov [the chief of staff of the Black Sea fleet] took upon himself the direction of the entire facility. And he determined never to surrender. Kornilov told his soldiers that 'If I myself give the order to retreat, kill me with your bayonets.' And of the soldiers he remarked 'Let the troops be first reminded of the word of God and then I will impart to them the word of the Tsar.'"

Russian vice admiral Kornilov defended Sebastopol during the Crimean War.

a joint naval and land bombardment of the city. They assumed the bombardment would destroy Sebastopol's defenses and permit the allied armies to enter the town and port.

The bombardment lasted three days. Each side scored a few lucky hits, and the casualty count mounted both in the trenches of the allies above Sebastopol and in the fortifications of the town itself.

Nothing went as planned on the allied side. As usual, the British and French military leaders failed to cooperate and coordinate their forces and their fleets. The French admiral decided that he did not have enough ammunition to carry out the bombardment for the stipulated period and ended his barrage of the port. The allied ships could not come in close enough to destroy the Russian guns along the wa-

---

Colonel Franz Edward Ivanovitch Todleben

Colonel Todleben probably possessed the best and most creative military mind of all those who fought in the Crimean War. William Howard Russell greatly appreciated his skills and describes some of Todleben's military thinking in General Todleben's History of the Defence of Sebastopol.

"On the 27th of September, when the Allies made their appearance, there were sixteen thousand men and thirty-two guns on the south side, and there were thirty-five hundred men on the north side and three thousand sailors on board the ships. Todleben, availing himself of the delay which took place on the part of the Allies, proceeded to fortify the place. The principle on which he proceeded, was to occupy the least extended position, and the nearest to the city, arm main points of the line with the most formidable artillery from the fleet, connect those points with trenches for musketry and enable separate batteries to concentrate powerful fire on the front and flank [of the enemy]."

Colonel Edward Todleben organized Sebastopol's citizens to build fortifications to resist an allied siege.

Allied troops pull artillery guns into place during the siege of Sebastopol. The initial siege lasted three days, giving the town time to regroup.

terfront in the harbor. Although they inflicted great damage on Sebastopol, the attack from the sea was a failure.

The French and British commands did not coordinate their efforts from the high land of Sebastopol. Although they agreed to keep firing together, a lucky Russian shot blew up a large French ammunition dump on October 18 and the French decided to halt their efforts. This was unfortunate because the British succeeded in making a large breach in the Redan Bastion. The Russian defenders fell back and the way was open to attack. Since the British had no plan to attack the Redan Bastion, however, they simply refused to take it any further. Another golden opportunity slipped through the hands of the allied command.

Meanwhile, between attacks, armies of Russian sailors, soldiers, and civilians worked frantically to fill the breaches in the defenses. In addition, Menshikov had returned to Sebastopol with his army on September 30, 1854, and his troops also took part in the nightly restoration of the

daily destruction. Then, inexplicably, after three days of shelling Sebastopol and causing great damage and loss of life to the enemy, the British and French called off the attack. Lord Cardigan was outraged at the operation. A *Times* correspondent reported that he heard Cardigan announce that "I have never in my life seen a siege conducted on such principles."[52]

Cardigan was right. The failed siege was due to a lack of understanding of how to conduct it. A siege involves completely encircling a town so that the occupants cannot leave and are unable to receive supplies. The objective is to capture the target following a tight, intense blockade and destructive bombardment resulting in a surrender or a successful assault on the position.

In order to be effective, the number of those besieging a position must be many times larger than those defending it. Besieging and attacking involve the loss of many more lives than defending a position.

In Sebastopol, the allied manpower did not even equal the defending Russian

An Englishman's View of the Siege

The Englishmen besieging Sebastopol knew how desperate the situation confronting them was in the fall of 1854. They had been told that the army would go into winter quarters and resume the campaign the following year but this did not happen. G. P. Evelyn, in A Diary of the Crimea, *discusses that siege.*

"We have done our worst and failed, and gradually we became alive to the undeniable fact that we were 'in a fix.' What can we do now? What shall we try next? These were the questions heard on all sides. 'We cannot long support this overwork—the dreadful trench duty. Our ranks must thin from day to day, as half rations and double duty fill our hospitals. And besides, it will always be necessary to keep the same amount of forces in the trenches, no matter how weak the regiments may become from which it is provided. This is really a bad look-out—the weaker we become in health and number, the more work will fall on us.'"

forces. During the siege, large numbers of Russian cavalry often simply left Sebastopol to go on patrol, or even to attack their besiegers. It appeared to journalist observers and to the soldiers themselves that the Russians controlled the situation and besieged the invading forces rather than the reverse.

In addition, not until late in the conflict did the British and French successfully block supplies going to Sebastopol. The Russian army obtained food, clothing, and replacement troops from two directions, overland from Ukraine and from the port of Kerch on the Sea of Azov. The allies simply made no effort to ambush these supplies while their own soldiers often went hungry.

Although the British accomplished none of the goals of the siege, they decided to continue it, in spite of the approach of winter in a desolate place, the weakness of their forces, their lack of supplies, and the

ever-growing size of the enemy force within Sebastopol. Nor did the alarming rate of disease among the troops dissuade the allies from remaining in the Crimea.

In the second thrust of the siege, soldiers worked relentlessly digging trenches from their own positions toward those of the Russian army. The nearer the trenches came to the Russian fortifications, the more deadly the allied attacks would be, the more accurate and persistent allied cannon fire.

The British soldiers who engaged in building and guarding the trenches knew the original siege plans had failed. One man wrote the following letter to his family on November 10:

It is generally understood that our siege operations have turned out a failure, that the town cannot be taken till regularly invested and attacked from the north side. Even if the French were to succeed in their attack and gain possession of the lower part of the town they could not hold it. We must rest on our arms till next spring and with immense reinforcements begin again.[53]

The Terrible Winter of 1854–1855

Through the terrible months of November and December 1854 and January and February of 1855 the exhausted British troops doggedly carried out the dangerous trenching activities. The snow piled up around them. The temperatures fell below freezing. Almost all the horses died. The British forces continued to decrease in size. The suffering of the few survivors of the original British became almost unendurable.

Similarly, on their front the French continued their own trenching toward the Russian fortifications. Unlike the British,

however, the French troops continued to receive reinforcements throughout the winter.

Fortunately for the British, Sardinian reinforcements from the Piedmont area arrived in January 1855 to join the allied side. Fifteen thousand Sardinian troops under General Alfonse Feraro Della Marmora put themselves under Raglan's command and took part in the attacks on the fortifications. This infusion of manpower enabled the British to continue to play a role in the Sebastopol campaign. Otherwise sheer numbers argued for the French to dominate the war effort; Emperor Napoleon himself at one point seriously intended to come to the Crimea to lead the allies in one last and decisive action.

While the allies inched their trenches through the frozen ground toward the Russian fortifications, the Russians were not idle. Colonel Todleben also worked feverishly. Night after night he encouraged his crews as they repaired breaches in the fortifications made by French and British fire during the previous day. Some

The Russians constructed these rope gauntlets to protect their gunners at Sebastopol.

Early Days of the Siege

"Down to the trenches, up in the morning, your rations, go and cut wood, fetch water, cook your food. Salt beef and pork with ship biscuit, in fact nothing else but ship rations, only no pea soup or in fact of anything but beef and biscuits, and sometimes a short supply of that. We get two glasses of rum daily and coffee, sugar and corn and rice when it can be provided. Mind you, we have to roast the coffee and pound it ourselves. I have not put a razor to my face since 12th August last. . . . I wish to God this was over."

of Todleben's methods were extraordinarily effective. He dug trenches to parallel those of the enemy. He constructed rifle pits outside the main line of defense. Those manning the pits constantly harassed the enemy diggers with rifle fire. He had his men listen, lying on the ground of their own tunnels, to the sounds of the enemy digging toward them. When he felt that the diggers were getting dangerously close, Todleben would send out his own sappers (demolition specialists) to blow up the enemy trenches and kill their occupants. The Russians also made frequent nighttime raids on the allied trenches farthest from the French and British encampments.

And so the endless pattern of trenching and the destruction of trenches, of bombardment and counterbombardment, continued during the terrible winter of 1854–1855. A British soldier wrote home:

We are prisoners in the little bit of ground we are encamped on; nothing to do, no change, no amusement, no books, only now and then a meal. However I pray God better times will come some day. Anything like common comfort would indeed appear sweet now. To be able to put clean things on, oh what a luxury it would be.[54]

His prayers finally were answered. Beginning in March 1855 conditions for the British began slowly to improve.

The government engineers arrived to begin work on the single-track military railroad. Gradually the train made its way up from Balaklava to the soldiers on the hills above Sebastopol. At long last supplies began to arrive in sufficient quantities to meet the needs of the half-starved troops. Additional British troops from India and China also came to the assistance of the besiegers of Sebastopol.

In April the allies prepared for a new bombardment of Sebastopol. Their spirits were buoyed by the extra rations, warm clothing and weather, and additional troop support. They hoped to open a large breach in the Russian fortifications through which they could launch a major offensive.

At long last Lord Raglan found support for an aggressive stance against the Russians in the person of yet another French commander in chief, General Aimable-Jean-Jacques Pélissier, a man with a face "something like a wild boar"[55] who replaced Canrobert. Although he weighed nearly three hundred pounds and had to be dragged around in a cart, Pélissier's mind remained nimble and sharp. As a result of this new cooperation, the two armies began an early April Sunday bombardment of the Russian fortifications.

For once the Russians were surprised by the suddenness and the length of the bombardment, which lasted ten days. The bombardment caused terrible destruction both in the Russian fortifications and to the town beyond. The allies lost sev-

General Aimable-Jean-Jacques-Pélissier (pictured) agreed with Lord Raglan that the allies should use aggressive tactics to oppose the Russians.

eral hundred troops, but the Russians, cramped in their fortifications, sustained at least five thousand casualties both from direct shelling and from falling debris of the forts. The April bombardment destroyed the Flagstaff Bastion on April 18. Unfortunately, the Russians mounted a successful counterattack before the British soldiers could seize their prize.

Bombardment and return fire continued throughout the spring as the weather grew warmer and the hills of the Crimea turned green. A series of additional attacks on the bastions in May was inconclusive although the allied guns inflicted more damage and continued to kill civilians within the port town. The Russians began to sustain very heavy casualties running into the thousands every week.

The Kerch Campaign

The British and French commands realized that as long as the Russians continued to get supplies, the siege might go on for years. So in May 1855 Lord Raglan and General Pélissier decided to send a small armada to Kerch, a Russian port on the Sea of Azov, in order to destroy one of the enemy's major supply lines.

In Paris, a disapproving Napoleon learned of these plans. He used a new invention, the telegraph, whose wires had just reached Constantinople, to send messages to Pélissier, ordering him to cease making naval preparations. But Pélissier decided to put the telegrams in his back pocket and went ahead with the joint British-French amphibious attack on Kerch.

The allies landed in Kerch on May 24, 1855, scattered the defending Russian forces, and then destroyed the swarm of undefended small supply ships in the Sea of Azov.

Clearly Pélissier was pleased with the results. He sent the following message to the war minister in Paris: "We have struck deep into the Russian resources; their chief line of supply is cut. I did well to carry out this expedition and I view with calm assurance the approach of the final act."[56]

Pélissier made an accurate assessment of the value of the mission, though he exaggerated the French role since most of the ships were British. Nevertheless, this one short, highly successful naval engagement helped to tighten the rope around the neck of the Russian army, even as the trenching toward Sebastopol continued at a snail's pace.

The British, French, and Sardinian forces together undertook several massive attacks on the Russian fortifications on June 6 and 7. They finally succeeded in capturing the dangerous Mamelon and Quarries positions, which the Russians had used successfully as protection for sharp-shooters who impeded the digging of the British trenching teams. The price was heavy. The French suffered 5,500 casualties and the British and Sardinians 670. Many soldiers at the time commented that the attack on the Mamelon was the French payback for not backing the British at the Alma in September 1854.

The Russians also sustained about five thousand casualties. The allies quickly took over these positions and prepared them to use as springboards for assaults on the remaining Russian forts. The allies were closing in on their enemy, but the human cost continued to rise as the area of the battle contracted.

On June 17, the allies again rained down death and destruction on the Russian fortifications and the civilians in the

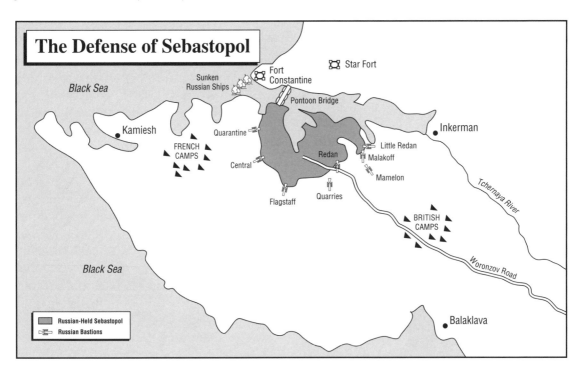

The Defense of Sebastopol

Black Sea

Sunken Russian Ships

Fort Constantine

Star Fort

Pontoon Bridge

Kamiesh

Quarantine

FRENCH CAMPS

Central

Flagstaff

Quarries

Redan

Little Redan

Malakoff

Mamelon

Inkerman

Tchernaya River

BRITISH CAMPS

Woronzov Road

Black Sea

Balaklava

Russian-Held Sebastopol
Russian Bastions

A photo dated June 7, 1855, shows allied leaders Lord Raglan, Omar Pasha, and General Pélissier discussing the siege of Sebastopol.

of debris. Yet no substantial gains were made in June 1855. Sebastopol held.

Lord Raglan, who had led the British forces since the beginning of the campaign, became ill and died on June 29 from dysentery and exhaustion. General James Simpson assumed command of the British forces. The siege continued.

And so it went . . . an endless, mind-numbing and deadly series of attacks and counterattacks. But by early summer it was clear that the loss of Kerch meant that the Russians would have to abandon Sebastopol. By May 1855 about 120,000 Russian troops were confined within the perimeter of the Sebastopol fortifications. After the allies cut the supply line from Kerch, the Russian government could not feed its army.

Tsar Nicholas too had died, on March 2, 1855, forming another reason to hope that the Russians would abandon Sebastopol. It was rumored in high government circles in St. Petersburg that his son and successor, Alexander II, was less warlike than his father. The allies hoped that the new tsar would continue the Crimean War for a short time out of filial loyalty and then find a way out of the conflict.

town. There were tremendously high losses, mounting to as many as a thousand a day, as masonry again fell on those within the doomed structures. Photographs show mounds of dead bodies under mountains

8 A Negotiated Peace: Losses and Gains

The result of this expedition was one of the most fruitless and lamentable that has ever occurred in the history of warfare.

—William Howard Russell

The new tsar did not want to dishonor his father's memory by abandoning Sebastopol immediately. He determined to launch one more attack against the invaders of his country. On August 16, 1855, sixty thousand Russian troops tried unsuccessfully to overtake the French and Sardinian positions by attacking along the Tchernaya River, which runs through the hills above the allied encampments.

In this action the British were onlookers. "We were merely spectators of the victory that was gained by the French and Sardinians over the Russians," Colonel Edward Hodge wrote home to his mother. The attack at the Tchernaya cost the Russians dearly. Hodge told his family the details:

> The Russians have, I believe lost quite 5,000 men, the allies about as many hundreds. A Russian general, N. A. Read, was killed and upon him was found the whole plan of attack. They were to have occupied the hills on our right, have cut off the Turkish army,

taken Balaclava, beaten up the English cavalry and some sixty guns, have burned all our shipping and then to have attacked and taken Kamiesch. Poor misguided people, they got beyond the first of our lines of defense and then they left some thousands dead, wounded or prisoners.[57]

The Russians Retreat

After the failure of his August offensive, Tsar Alexander decided to evacuate Sebastopol. The French trenches were within twenty-five yards of the Malakoff Bastion. Hand-to-hand combat took place daily. General Gorchakov, now head of the army defending Sebastopol, told the tsar that the Malakoff was in danger of capture and that if he lost the Malakoff he could no longer hold his position. The tsar knew that the south side of Sebastopol lay in ruins. The Russians would go.

They burned what they could and then left. On the night of September 10, 1855, the Russian army crossed over to the north side of Sebastopol on pontoon bridges they had been constructing for some time. To the allies they left the burned-out ruin of what had been the southern side of the fortress and naval base of Sebastopol.

"Quite a Different Place"

The Crimean War did not end with the fall of Sebastopol. Sporadic fighting continued for the next several months. There were no more major military encounters. The combatants now struggled to find a way of ending the war that everyone had grown weary of fighting.

By the time Sebastopol fell the British army numerically resembled the original army that left England in 1854. It had taken the British a long time to reconstitute its army because of the government's policy of keeping only limited reserve units.

Finally, on November 9, 1855, Sir William Codrington took command of an army of almost forty thousand troops. Few of these soldiers were veterans of the first army. They could not imagine the horrors their predecessors had experienced.

One survivor, Little Hodge, reflected on the differences between the accommodations of the army of 1855 and of 1854:

The camps are so changed I hardly could recognize them; such roads, such stacks of wood, corn and stores of all sorts, railway, stone cottages, huts etc.

A retreating Russian soldier looks back at the burning town of Sebastopol as villagers and soldiers hurriedly evacuate.

quite a different place to what it was. The absence of vultures strikes me. Last year there were hundreds.[58]

Still, the British army had to endure yet another Russian winter before the war officially ended.

An Ultimatum

Tsar Alexander II had nothing to gain by continuing the war. But he knew that once he admitted defeat, his country would be compelled to make considerable concessions. Finally, the allies enlisted the diplomatic aid of the Austrian Empire to bring an end to the conflict.

Austria had not fought in the war. Clearly, however, she had good reason to wish it to stop. Austrian leaders knew that continued political unrest in Europe would endanger their own internal stability. So the Austrian emperor, Franz Joseph, sent an ultimatum to Tsar Alexander II demanding that he agree to end the Crimean War. Finally Alexander gave in to international pressure and he accepted unconditional surrender terms on January 26, 1856.

The Treaty of Paris

Leaders of the allies and the Russians met in Paris on March 25, 1856, to negotiate fi-

An allied encampment outside Sebastopol in 1855 shows the benefits of improved supplies. By the end of the war, troops' accommodations were vastly different from the deplorable living conditions early on.

Allied and Russian leaders meet in Paris in 1856 to negotiate peace terms. The conference resulted in the Treaty of Paris.

nal peace terms. It was significant that the congress took place in Paris rather than London, whose government had originally led the alliance against Russia. The selection of Paris as the site of the conference indicated that Napoleon III had gained his primary objective of achieving a place of importance in European diplomacy even before the countries of Europe signed the peace treaty.

The conference lasted only a few days, concluding with the Treaty of Paris on March 30. This treaty contained some very important terms. Among the most significant were those clauses that guaranteed the independence of Turkey and ensured that Russian warships would have to stay out of the Black Sea, which was declared a neutral body of water. This meant that Russia no longer dominated the Black Sea and for the moment did not pose a threat to British interests in the Mediterranean Sea. However, since Turkey still controlled the Dardanelles it could send in ships to police the Black Sea for violations of the peace treaty.

As a result of the peace treaty Turkey had to recognize the right of its Christian inhabitants to practice their religious customs. In addition, all countries could navigate the Danube River freely. Russia lost some territory she previously controlled in Bessarabia and could not rebuild Sebastopol as a naval base.

The Sardinians achieved some of their own objectives. In exchange for their

Prime Minister Conte di Cavour of Sardinia used the conference at Paris as a forum to complain about the Austrian Empire's rule of his nation.

military efforts during the war, they earned the opportunity to speak at the peace conference. There Conte di Cavour, prime minister of Sardinia, aired his grievances against what he considered to be the authoritarian rule of the Austrian Empire over lands in which Italian people lived. This was an important step on the road toward achieving Italian independence, which came to fruition in 1871.

Curiously, although the war began over disputes in Palestine, the issue of jurisdiction over Holy Land shrines was addressed by no one at the Paris peace conference.

Outcomes of the War

And so ended the Crimean War. It had lasted for twenty-eight months. Nearly half a million fatalities had occurred in all theaters of the war, including those men who died on the battlefield, in hospitals, and at sea. Fully two-thirds of the deaths resulted from disease, starvation, and exposure. Well over one hundred thousand men died during the siege of Sebastopol alone.

The financial cost of the war was equally staggering. Britain spent £69 million, France £93 million, and Russia £142 million to wage war.

Clearly Napoleon III saw his political star rising in European affairs. Because he was so successful during the Crimean War, he came to believe that he could play a major role in future events, and he certainly wanted to extend French power. Unfortunately for France and Napoleon, the French emperor lacked the skills to fulfill his dreams and he did not realize his limitations. He continued to be distrusted by

European leaders and his continued diplomatic activities were viewed as transparent attempts to increase French power in Europe.

The Crimean War had a great impact on the British government and the British people. The government felt humiliated by the terrible incompetence of its officers and by the demonstration in public of its military ineptitude. Slowly Britain began to overhaul its military, making it increasingly difficult for such incompetents as Lucan and Cardigan to command troops. And a new system of promotion by examination now made it more likely that men of ability from the middle classes also could have a chance to advance in the military services.

There were other, less hopeful, effects in Britain. Throughout most of the nineteenth century, England, often working with Russia, had acted as the sentinels of the European continent. They wished to keep control of their respective territories. The Crimean War, however, made many people in Britain rethink the country's role in Europe, particularly its role as a military power. Increasing sums were spent on the British navy and the empire seemed to be the major consideration of British foreign policy. The partnership with Russia was seriously damaged. During this period of British inattention to European affairs, other, less stable governments began to look for opportunities to grab additional land.

Sardinians learned the lesson that the cause of Italian unity could benefit from the troubles of other countries. Her leaders therefore looked forward to other opportunities to advance Italian interests during wartime.

British Anger with Lack of Prussian Support

The following excerpt from a letter written by Prince Albert, quoted by Cecil Woodham-Smith in Queen Victoria from Her Birth to the Death of the Prince Consort, *reflects the British reluctance to have Prussia represented at the Paris peace conference.*

"As for the special claims of Prussia to take part in the negotiations, these have no sort of foundation. It is not revenge which prevents us from admitting them, for this would be childish, but over and above the justifiable fear of increasing the number of our opponents in the approaching discussions, we are actuated by the conviction that it would be a most perilous precedent for the future to admit the principle, that Power may take part in the great game of politics without having laid down their stake. What right then, have others to interfere, who have taken no part in the conflict, and have constantly maintained that their interests are not touched by the matter in dispute and that therefore they would not take any part in the business?"

Russia was the chief loser in the Crimean War. She lost territory, prestige, as well as her faith in the European state system to settle international disputes diplomatically. Its leaders chafed under the terms of the Treaty of Paris. So, like many Italian leaders, the tsar and his advisers now hoped that another European crisis might afford them an opportunity to recover their losses.

A Treaty Violation

Russia's opportunity for revenge came a mere fourteen years later. Prussia successfully fought a series of wars, defeating France and Austria. Italy took advantage of European instability to obtain land from Austria and become the kingdom of Italy. Russia did not come to the assistance of Austria because of its involvement in the ending of the Crimean War. Instead, Russia, like Sardinia, took advantage of the situation to fulfill its own ambitions.

In 1871 Russia renounced the Treaty of Paris, particularly its Black Sea clauses. It declared that henceforth Russian ships again would sail on the Black Sea. In 1871 no power in Europe rose to denounce this clear violation of international law. The European community and a sense of responsibility for maintaining it had weakened.

Alexander II's defeat in the Crimean War took both territory and prestige from Russia.

So, a mere fourteen years after the signing of the Treaty of Paris, Europe was politically more unstable than it had been in 1854. This instability became a hallmark of Europe in the second half of the nineteenth century. Certainly the Crimean War cannot be blamed for the discord that marked this period of European history. But the war can be identified as the point at which the countries of Europe started dealing with one another in substantially different ways from the first half of the nineteenth century.

Notes

Introduction: The Setting

1. Quoted in Alexis S. Troubetzkoy, *The Crimean War: A Russian Chronicle.* New York: St. Martin's Press, 1977, p. 33.

Chapter 1: The Origins of the Crimean War

2. Alan Warwick Palmer, *The Banner of Battle: The Story of the Crimean War.* New York: St. Martin's Press, 1987, p. 19.

3. Quoted in General Sir Edward Hamley, *The War in the Crimea.* London: Seeley, 1910, p. 8.

4. Quoted in Palmer, *The Banner of Battle,* p. 19.

5. Quoted in Hamley, *The War in the Crimea,* p. 17.

6. Alexis S. Troubetzkoy, *The Road to Balaklava.* Toronto: Trafalgar Press, 1986, p. 110.

Chapter 2: Armies and War Preparations

7. Peter Gibbs, *Crimean Blunder.* London: Frederick Muller, 1960, p. 78.

8. Christopher Hibbert, *The Destruction of Lord Raglan: A Tragedy of the Crimean War, 1854–1855.* London: Longmans, 1961, p. 241.

9. Daniel Lysons, *The Crimean War from First to Last.* London: John Murray, 1895, p. 15.

10. Palmer, *The Banner of Battle,* p. 74.

11. Gibbs, *Crimean Blunder,* p. 105.

Chapter 3: To the Alma and Beyond

12. Gibbs, *Crimean Blunder,* p. 134.

13. Palmer, *The Banner of Battle,* p. 94.

14. Gibbs, *Crimean Blunder,* p. 136.

15. Quoted in Albert Seaton, *The Crimean War: A Russian Chronicle.* New York: St. Martin's Press, 1977, p. 83.

16. Cecil Woodham-Smith, *The Reason Why.* New York: McGraw-Hill, 1960, pp. 181–82.

Chapter 4: The Battle of Balaklava

17. Woodham-Smith, *The Reason Why,* p. 130.

18. Quoted in A. W. Kinglake, *The Invasion of the Crimea: Its Origins, and an Account of Its Progress Down to the Death of Lord Raglan.* London: William Blackwood and Sons, 1877, p. 80.

19. Quoted in Hibbert, *The Destruction of Lord Raglan,* p. 135.

20. John Sweetman, *Balaclava, 1854.* London: Osprey, 1990, p. 57.

21. Quoted in Woodham-Smith, *The Reason Why,* p. 87.

22. John Selby, *The Thin Red Line of Balaclava.* London: Hamish Hamilton, 1970, p. 67.

23. Quoted in Gibbs, *Crimean Blunder,* p. 214.

24. Kinglake, *The Invasion of the Crimea,* p. 220.

25. William Howard Russell, *General Todleben's History of the Defence of Sebastopol, 1854–5.* London: Tinsley Brothers, 1865, p. 220.

Chapter 5: The Battle of Inkerman

26. Quoted in Russell, *General Todleben's History,* p. 124.

27. Quoted in Marquess of Anglesey, ed., *'Little Hodge,' Being Extracts from the Diaries and Letters of Colonel Edward Cooper Hodge Written During the Crimean War, 1854–1856.* London: Leo Cooper, 1971, p. 54.

28. Hibbert, *The Destruction of Lord Raglan,* p. 170.

29. Quoted in Selby, *The Thin Red Line of Balaclava,* p. 178.

30. Hibbert, *The Destruction of Lord Raglan,* p. 170.

Chapter 6: Life in the War Zone

31. Quoted in Woodham-Smith, *The Reason Why,* p. 178.

32. Hibbert, *The Destruction of Lord Raglan*, p. 30.

33. Palmer, *The Banner of Battle*, p. 143.

34. Quoted in John Black Atkins, *The Life of Sir William Howard Russell*, vol. 1. London: John Murray, 1911, p. 133.

35. Quoted in Woodham-Smith, *The Reason Why*, p. 192.

36. Palmer, *The Banner of Battle*, p. 142.

37. Quoted in Cecil Woodham-Smith, *Florence Nightingale*. New York: Atheneum, 1951, p. 225.

38. Quoted in Palmer, *The Banner of Battle*, p. 142.

39. Quoted in Hibbert, *The Destruction of Lord Raglan*, p. 247.

40. Quoted in C. E. Vulliamy, *Crimea: The Campaign of 1854–1856*. London: Jonathan Cape, l939, p. 13.

41. Quoted in Hibbert, *The Destruction of Lord Raglan*, p. 236.

42. Hibbert, *The Destruction of Lord Raglan*, p. 202.

43. Quoted in Anglesey, *'Little Hodge,'* p. 57.

44. Quoted in Anglesey, *'Little Hodge,'* p. 57.

45. Quoted in Atkins, *The Life of Sir William Howard Russell*, p. 202.

46. Quoted in Anglesey, *'Little Hodge,'* p. 71.

47. Palmer, *The Banner of Battle*, p. 174.

Chapter 7: The Siege of Sebastopol

48. Woodham-Smith, *The Reason Why*, p. 191.

49. Quoted in Selby, *The Thin Red Line of Balaclava*, p. 87.

50. Russell, *General Todleben*, p. 116.

51. George Palmer Evelyn, *A Diary of the Crimea*. London: Gerald Duckworth, 1954, p. 122.

52. Quoted in Cecil Woodham-Smith, *The Reason Why*, p. 286.

53. Quoted in Palmer, *The Banner of Battle*, p. 187.

54. Evelyn, *A Diary of the Crimea*, p. 108.

55. Palmer, *The Banner of Battle*, p. 188.

56. Quoted in Archibald Forbes, *The Life of Napoleon the Third*. New York: Dodd, Mead, 1897, p. 188.

Chapter 8: A Negotiated Peace: Losses and Gains

57. Quoted in Anglesey, *'Little Hodge,'* p. 124.

58. Quoted in Anglesey, *'Little Hodge,'* p. 137.

For Further Reading

George Palmer Evelyn, *A Diary of the Crimea.* London: Gerald Duckworth, 1954. An account of a soldier's suffering during the war.

General Sir Edward Hamley, *The War in the Crimea.* London: Seeley, 1910. Very readable account of the events leading up to and associated with the Crimean War, from the perspective of an English officer.

John Selby, *The Thin Red Line of Balaclava.* London: Hamish Hamilton, 1970. Based on the diaries of participants in the war and filled with colorful, poignant details of the bravery, heroism, and individual suffering of both men and mounts.

Evelyn E. P. Tisdall, *Restless Consort.* London: Stanley Paul, 1952. Readable account of the role that Albert, the Prince Consort, played in English affairs during this period.

Cecil Woodham-Smith, *Florence Nightingale.* New York: Atheneum, 1951. Very detailed account of the private and public turmoils of the nurse who brought solace and the light of rationality to the treatment of British soldiers in military hospitals.

Works Consulted

Marquess of Anglesey, ed., *'Little Hodge,' Being Extracts from the Diaries and Letters of Colonel Edward Cooper Hodge Written During the Crimean War, 1854–1856.* London: Leo Cooper, 1971. Wonderful diary, written by a cavalry officer, that covers the entire two years of the war as seen from the trenches and the mud.

John Black Atkins, *The Life of Sir William Howard Russell.* Vol. 1. London: John Murray, 1911. Contains much useful information regarding the role played by the first special correspondent of the *Times* of London in alerting the English public to the horrors associated with the Crimean War.

Diplomatic Study on the Crimean War (1852–1856). Vol. 1. London: W. H. Allen, 1882. An official report of the Russian government; contains information on the negotiations among the European powers with interests in Turkey that were being threatened.

Archibald Forbes, *The Life of Napoleon the Third.* New York: Dodd, Mead, 1897. Provides useful information, placing the Crimean War within the context of Napoleon's overall foreign policy.

Peter Gibbs, *Crimean Blunder.* London: Frederick Muller, 1960. A delightful book written by an Englishman who sees the actors and actions of the Crimean War as foolish in the extreme, and the war as avoidable.

David M. Goldfrank, *The Origins of the Crimean War.* London: Longman, 1994. Account of the political background to the Crimean War.

Constantin de Grunwald, *Tzar Nicholas I.* New York: Macmillan, 1955. Short account of the reign of Nicholas I with many quotations from people who served the tsar.

Christopher Hibbert, *The Destruction of Lord Raglan: A Tragedy of the Crimean War, 1854–1855.* London: Longman, 1961. Excellent portrayal of Lord Raglan as a thoughtful, hardworking, misunderstood man whose failures in the Crimea were as much the fault of an unreformed military system as they were a result of Raglan's own limitations.

Blanchard Jerrold, *The Life of Napoleon III.* Vol. 4. London: Longman's, Green, 1882. Old-fashioned account of the life of Napoleon III, based on state records and personal accounts by his contemporaries. Sheds some interesting light on French involvement in the Crimean War.

A. W. Kinglake, *The Invasion of the Crimea: Its Origins, and an Account of Its Progress Down to the Death of Lord Raglan.* London: William Blackwood and Sons, 1877. The most important early account of the events of the Crimean War, written by a war correspondent.

Andrew D. Lambert, *The Crimean War: British Grand Strategy, 1853–56.* Manchester:

Manchester University Press, 1990. Describes the war as a worldwide conflict, involving not only events in the Black Sea, but also in the Pacific Ocean, the Baltic Sea, and in Asia.

W. Bruce Lincoln, *Nicholas I: Emperor and Autocrat of All the Russians.* Bloomington: University of Indiana Press, 1980. Describes the inflexibility of the tsar and the political system he created and suggests that these traits and the regimentation of a backward country contributed to Russia's loss in the Crimean War.

Daniel Lysons, *The Crimean War from First to Last.* London: John Murray, 1895. Delightful series of letters from a general officer back to family in London, showing growing disgust with lack of insight and lack of planning for the British army in the Crimea.

B. Kingsley Martin, *The Triumph of Lord Palmerston.* London: George Allen & Unwin, 1924. A study of public opinion in England that led to that country's decision to lend assistance to Turkey in 1854.

Alan Warwick Palmer, *The Banner of Battle: The Story of the Crimean War.* New York: St. Martin's Press, 1987. Account of the Crimean War from the perspective of recent understanding of the relationships between the belligerents in the mid-1850s.

William Howard Russell, *General Todleben's History of the Defence of Sebastopol, 1854–5.* London: Tinsley Brothers, 1865. An insightful explanation of the defenses of Sebastopol according to the Russian engineer who built the fortifications around the naval base.

Albert Seaton, *The Crimean War: A Russian Chronicle.* New York: St. Martin's Press, 1977. Discusses the origins and events of the Crimean War from the perspective of the tsar of Russia and the military and political leaders of the tsar's government.

Anthony Sterling, *The Story of the Highland Brigade in the Crimea.* London: Hastings House, 1895. Provides details of the actions involving the 93rd Highland Regiment, based on a series of letters from soldiers during the war.

John Sweetman, *Balaclava, 1854.* London: Osprey, 1990. Part of Osprey's military campaigns series; contains extremely useful maps showing dispositions of the British, French, Russian, and Turkish armies.

Harold Temperley, *England and the Near East.* London: Longman's, Green, 1936. Extremely detailed account of the diplomatic exchanges that led to the outbreak of the Crimean War.

Alexis S. Troubetzkoy, *The Crimean War: A Russian Chronicle.* New York: St. Martin's Press, 1977. Provides a view of the Crimean War from a Russian perspective.

Alexis S. Troubetzkoy, *The Road to Balaklava.* Toronto: Trafalgar Press, 1986. Describes the many political mistakes and misunderstandings that led to the onset of the Crimean War.

C. E. Vulliamy, *Crimea: The Campaign of 1854–1856.* London: Jonathan Cape,

1939. Well-balanced account that updates earlier accounts by Crimean War participants.

Philip Warner, *The Fields of War: A Young Cavalryman's Crimean Campaign*. London: John Murray, 1977. The edited collected letters of Temple Goodman, a cavalry officer who survived the Crimean campaign and wrote letters to his family describing his experiences.

David Wetzel, *The Crimean War: A Diplomatic History*. New York: Columbia University Press, 1985. Sketches the involvement of the major European diplomatic leaders in the crisis in Turkey and their inability to find a way to avoid war.

Cecil Woodham-Smith, *Queen Victoria from Her Birth to the Death of the Prince Consort*. New York: Knopf, 1972. Full of details regarding the childhood, marriage, and family life of Queen Victoria.

Cecil Woodham-Smith, *The Reason Why*. New York: McGraw-Hill, 1960. Wonderfully rich, colorful account of one of history's most famous cavalry charges. Full of details regarding the personalities of the British military leaders, whose mutual dislikes led to the destruction of the Light Brigade.

Index

Abdul Medjid (sultan of Turkey), 11, 14
Aberdeen, earl of, 29, 71
Airey, Sir Richard, 52
Albert, Prince, 97
Alexander II (tsar of Russia), 91–92, 94
Alma. *See* Battle of the Alma

Battle of the Alma, 35–44
  British advance to, 33–35
  casualties, 40
  map, 40
  Russian defeat at, 39–41
Battle of Balaklava, 44–56
  attack on the redoubts, 44–46
  map, 47
  Balaklava Plain map, 45
  casualties at, 51, 55
  charge of Heavy Brigade, 49–52
  map, 50
  charge of Light Brigade, 52–55

map, 54
preparations for defense, 44–45
redoubts at, 44–46
retreat of Russian cavalry, 48–49
Battle of Inkerman, 57–66
  British positions, 57–58
  first contact, 60–61
  French join battle, 63
  map, 65
  Menshikov's plan, 59–60
  results of battle, 65–66
  Russian withdrawal, 64–65
  tsar's ultimatum to Menshikov, 58–59
Bosquet, Pierre, 35
Britain
  advance to Alma, 33–35
  advance to Sebastopol, 40–42
  animosity among cavalry leaders, 34
  declared war on Russia, 18–19
  feared Napoleon III,

27–28
  first attack, 28–32
  no clear plan of engagement, 26–27
  port of supply, 42
  prewar army, 23–25
  prewar political maneuvering, 12–17
  sorry state of hospitals in, 69–70
  starvation and suffering of soldiers, 74–78
    improvement in diet, 78–79
  see also named battles
Brown, Sir George, 26, 36
Budenell, Lord, 27

Cambridge, duke of, 36, 39, 62
Campbell, Sir Colin, 35, 37, 45, 47–48
Canning, Sir Stafford, 13–14
Canrobert, François-Certain, 43, 65, 89
Cardigan, Lord, 27, 34, 47, 52, 55, 85

casualties
  at the Alma, 40
  at Balaklava, 51, 55
  disease as major
    killer, 28–29,
    68–69
  at Inkerman, 64–65
  at Sebastopol, 90
Cathcart, Sir George,
  46, 62, 81
Cavour, conte di
  (prime minister of
  Sardinia), 96
Clarendon, Lord, 14
Codrington, Sir
  William, 36, 93
Crimean peninsula,
  map, 31
Crimean War
  disease as major
    killer in, 28–29,
    68–69
  first allied attack,
    28–32
  hurricane during,
    76–78
  important dates, 8
  international stage of,
    map, 17
  negotiated peace,
    92–97
  origins of, 11–19
  outcomes of, 96–98
  Palestine disputes as
    cause of, 11–13
  Treaty of Paris,
    94–96

see also Battle of the
  Alma; Battle of
  Inkerman; Se-
  bastopol, siege
  and defense

Daily News (London),
  78
Dannenberg, P. A., 59,
  63–64
Davis, Elizabeth,
  73–74
Delane, John, 70–71
disease, as major killer,
  28–29, 68–69

Elliot, Alexander James
  Hardy, 49–50
Elton, John, 63
Evelyn, George Palmer,
  83, 86

Feraro Della Marmora,
  Alfonse, 87
Fielder (British
  general), 29
Fischer, Coronet, 80
France
  advantages in war
    zone, 67–68
  benefits from the war,
    95–96
  capitalized on Russo-
    Turkey crisis, 15–16
  declared war on
    Russia, 18–19
  failed support at

Alma, 40
  first attack, 28–32
  joined battle at
    Inkerman, 63
  no clear plan of
    engagement, 26–27
  prewar army, 23
Franz Joseph (emperor
  of Austria), 94

Gorchakov, Paul, 59,
  65, 92
Gordon, Alexander, 29,
  66
Great Elchi. See
  Canning, Sir
  Stafford
Great Redoubt, 33,
  35–37

Hall, John, 71–72
Hamilton-Gordon,
  George (earl of
  Aberdeen), 29, 71
Heavy Brigade
  charge of, 49–52
  map, 50
Herbert, Sir Sidney, 71,
  73, 78
Hodge, Edward
  Cooper, 32, 92
Hodge, Little, 93
horses, suffering of,
  76
hurricane, 76–78

important dates, 8

Inkerman. *See* Battle of Inkerman

Kerch campaign, 89–91
Kiriakov, V. I., 35
Kornilov (Russian admiral), 83

Lady with the Lamp. *See* Nightingale, Florence
Light Brigade
  charge of, 52–55
  map, 54
Liprandi, Pavel, 45, 59
Lucan, Lord, 29, 32, 34, 45–46, 52
Lyons, Sir Edmund, 31, 43

Manchester Guardian, 78
maps
  attack on the re-doubts (Balaklava), 47
  Balaklava Plain, 45
  Battle of the Alma, 40
  Battle of Inkerman, 65
  charge of Heavy Brigade, 50
  charge of Light Brigade, 54
  Crimean peninsula, 31
  defense of Sebastopol, 90

international stage of Crimean War, 17
Marx, Karl, 30
Medjid, Abdul (sultan of Turkey), 11, 14
Menshikov, Aleksandr (prince of Russia), 20, 56
  at Alma, 32–35, 37–38
  chosen to command troops, 13–14
  description of, 38
  failed to attack before Sebastopol, 42–43
  as observer at Inkerman, 64
  plan at Inkerman, 59–60
  tsar's ultimatum to, 58–59
Michael (grand duke of Russia), 58
Moller, F. F. von, 59
Morning Herald (London), 78

Nakhimov, Paul, 17–18
Napoleon I (emperor of France), 37
Napoleon III (emperor of France), 15, 58, 67, 87, 89
  benefits from the war, 95–96
  feared by British, 27–28

newspapers. *See named papers;* press
Nicholas (grand duke of Russia), 58
Nicholas I (tsar of Russia), 9, 37
  death of, 91
  preparations and invasion, 12–15
  ultimatum to Menshikov, 58–59
Nightingale, Florence, 71–74, 78
Nolan, Lewis Edward, 35, 52, 53, 55
nurses, in Crimea, 71–74, 78

Paget, Sir George, 47
Palestine, disputes over, as early cause of war, 11–13
Panmure, Lord, 78
Pasha, Omar, 22
Pélissier, Aimable-Jean-Jacques, 89–90
Pennefather, Sir John, 62
photographers. *See* press
press
  impact on war, 25–26, 70–71
  see also Times (London)

Raglan, Lord, 29–30

at Alma, 34–35, 40
at Balaklava, 48–49,
    52, 55
commanded British
    troops, 23–24
death, 91
at Inkerman, 60–61,
    63, 65
lack of strategic
    planning by, 43
prepares defense of
    Balaklava, 43–45
at Sebastopol, 80, 87,
    89
Read, N. A., 92
redoubt(s)
    at Balaklava, 44–46
    defined, 44
    Great Redoubt, 33,
        35–37
Reform Club, 78
reporters. *See* press
Richard, William, 75
Russell, William
    Howard, 56, 70, 77
Russia
    causes of war and, 12
    invasion of Turkey,
        14–15
    massacre of Sinope,
        17–19
    missed opportunity
        early, 31–32
    prewar army of,
        20–22
    prewar demands on
        Turkey, 13–14

privation of soldiers,
    75
violated Treaty of
    Paris, 98
war declared against,
    18–19
see also Menshikov,
    Aleksandr; *named
    battles*

Saint-Arnaud, Le Roy
    de, 23, 29–30, 34–35,
    40, 80
Scarlett, Sir James, 47,
    49–51
Sebastopol, siege and
    defense, 80–91
    casualties, 90
    first bombardment,
        83–87
    flank march around,
        80–81
    heavy French losses at
        Mamelon, 90
    Kerch campaign,
        89–91
    map, 90
    Russian prepara-
        tions for defense,
        81–83
    terrible winter,
        87–89
Select Committee on
    the Army, 74
Shegog (orderly), 50
"sick man of Europe,"
    11–12

Simpson, James, 91
Sinope, Russian
    massacre at, 17–19
smoke, important role
    at the Alma, 36
Soimonov, F. I., 62
Somerset, Fitzroy. *See*
    Raglan, Lord
Soyer, Alexis, 78–79
*Soyer's Culinary
    Campaign*, 79
starvation and suffering
    of soldiers, 74–78
    improvement in diet,
        78–79
Strangeways (British
    general), 62

telegraph, available
    only late in war, 25,
    89
Tennyson, Alfred Lord,
    20, 44
Times (London), 27, 56,
    70–72, 78, 85
Tiutcheva, Anna F., 12
Todleben, Franz
    Edward Ivanovitch,
    61
    brilliant defense of
        Sebastopol by,
        81–84, 87–88
Treaty of Paris, 94–96
    violated by Russia,
        98
Trevelyan, Sir George,
    11

Turkey
  heavy losses at Bala-
    klava, 46
  invasion by Russia,
    14–15
  massacre at Sinope by
    Russia, 17–19
  prewar army of,
    22–23
  Russia's demands on,
    13–14
  as "sick man of
    Europe," 11–12

Victoria (queen of
  England), 16, 39, 71

war correspondents. *See*
  press
Wellington, duke of,
  24, 37

Picture Credits

Cover photo: Giraudon/Art Resource, NY

Archive Photos, 13, 14, 37, 58, 89

Corbis-Bettmann, 62, 68, 79, 83, 93

Imperial War Museum/Archive Photos, 42, 87

Library of Congress, 10, 12, 16, 25, 55, 71, 73, 74, 78, 82, 85, 91, 94, 96

Peter Newark's Military Pictures, 21, 23, 26, 51, 52

North Wind Picture Archives, 98

Jeff Paris, 22, 24, 48, 84, 95

Popperfoto/Archive Photos, 60, 70

Springer/Corbis-Bettmann, 57

Stock Montage, Inc., 18, 28, 38, 39, 41, 64, 65, 69, 77

About the Author

Deborah Bachrach was born and raised in New York City, where she received her undergraduate education. She earned a Ph.D. in history from the University of Minnesota. Dr. Bachrach has taught at the University of Minnesota as well as at St. Francis College, Joliet, Illinois, and Queens College, the City University of New York. In addition, she has worked for many years in the fields of medical research and public policy development. She also teaches English as a second language to the many recent foreign arrivals to the Midwest, where she makes her home.